On the Way
with Jesus

On the Way with Jesus

A PASSION FOR MISSION

Richard Showalter

Foreword by Ralph D. Winter

Herald Press
Scottdale, Pennsylvania
Waterloo, Ontario

Library of Congress Cataloging-in-Publication Data
Showalter, Richard.
On the way with Jesus : a passion for mission / Richard Showalter.
    p. cm.
ISBN 978-0-8361-9415-9 (pbk.)
1. Missions. I. Title.
BV2061.3.S56 2008
266–dc22

                                2008004227

ON THE WAY WITH JESUS
Copyright © 2008 by Herald Press, Scottdale, Pa. 15683
  Published simultaneously in Canada by Herald Press,
  Waterloo, Ont. N2L 6H7. All rights reserved
Library of Congress Catalog Card Number: 2008004227
International Standard Book Number: 978-0-8361-9415-9
Printed in the United States of America
Cover by Greg Yoder
The 10/40 Window graphic on page 94 by Joseph Hollinger

13 12 11 10 09   10 9 8 7 6 5 4 3 2

To order or request information please call 1-800-245-7894 or visit www.heraldpress.com.

*To the thousands of faithful witnesses from Anabaptist congregations
—past, present, and future—
serving on six continents with Eastern Mennonite Missions,
Mennonite Brethren Missions and Service International, the
Mennonite Mission Network, Rosedale Mennonite Missions, Canada
Witness, Brethren in Christ World Missions,
and other mission societies from North America alongside their
partners in mission from Europe and the Global South*

CONTENTS

FOREWORD

This little book is simply incredible. It is jammed with fascinating anecdotes, irrefutable facts, wise judgment, and the handling of very delicate issues with phenomenal wisdom.

I have for many years known that my own Presbyterian evangelicalism has gained whatever unique vitality it has from Anabaptist sources. Throughout many years of teaching the story of God's expanding will in our world across its many centuries, I have constantly taught that evangelicalism, which is controlled by no one denomination, is nevertheless the outworking of that virile, undefeatable Anabaptist tradition. It is not just Anabaptists who know that.

This book will be a treasure for Anabaptists, of course. It should rightly be an even greater surprise and pleasure for those of us who have not grown up in that sturdy movement and have so much to learn from people who have taken the Bible more seriously than any theological tradition.

What a marvel that so much of so great value to global Christian responsibility, challenge, and perspective could have been packed into so small a book. Nevertheless, it is amazingly comprehensive, and its text girdles the globe.

The really nice thing is that while it is considerably and helpfully beamed to younger people, it yet carries many weighty insights with ease.

This gem deserves a wide hearing. My hope and prayer is that it will in fact be widely used.

Ralph D. Winter
Frontier Mission Fellowship
Pasadena, California
May 2008

INTRODUCTION

Behold, I have set before you an open door.
—Revelation 3:8 (RSV)

The world is no stranger to closed doors. Repeatedly throughout history, doors have slammed shut—doors for progress, development, communication, travel. A large percentage of the world's population from time immemorial has been curtailed in its opportunities for normal human expression and development by doors that have remained locked through oppression, violence, greed, and the chaos of conflict.

But one door has remained open. The door for sharing the good news of freedom in Jesus Christ has never been closed since Pentecost. For no matter how many barriers are erected to inhibit the freedom of the people of God, the gospel breaks forth in new forms and configurations beyond the barriers. God is at work everywhere, drawing people to the risen Christ. In prisons, on slave ships, in forced detentions, and in the freedom of natural human interchanges, the good news has continued to travel.

Yet there are eras when the door seems to swing open even more widely. In the providence of God, we live in one such era. It is a season not unlike the time of Jesus and Paul, when the *pax Romana* (peace of Rome) created conditions for easy transportation and communication all around the Mediterranean Sea.

Today we too travel and communicate with unprecedented ease, using technologies that would have astounded our ancestors only a hundred years ago.

And there is traffic through the open door! The world's most viewed motion picture, the *Jesus* film, is being seen by people in hundreds of languages and people groups. Radio waves are filled with programs in dozens of languages beamed to every corner of the globe, announcing the peace of Christ. Relief, development, and microfinance workers are everywhere offering assistance in the name of Christ. A higher percentage of the world's population than ever before are serious Christians. Entire nations are being impacted.

Yet our Lord still beckons us to the frontiers. Dozens of world-class cities (cities with more than one million people) are without significant Christian presence. Thousands of people groups have no viable church. Tens of thousands of clans and family webs have not encountered the Christ who transforms.

As North American Christians, we speak the trade language of the world. The most advanced technology in human history is at our fingertips. We have the wealth to use it.

But will we place our lives and our possessions at the disposal of Christ? Will we walk through the open door God has set before us? Or will we build bigger and bigger barns, committed to our own security rather than to the peace of Christ?

"Behold, I have set before you an open door." In the simple obedience of faith, we will walk through it.

PART 1

THE VISION

THE MISSION OF JESUS

A buzzword in Anabaptist and evangelical circles since the end of World War II has been "recovering the vision"—a vision for reconnecting with the spiritual dynamic of our sixteenth-century forebears. Those Anabaptists were a covenant community in mission, committed to radical faithfulness to Jesus.

When Bishop Lesslie Newbigin returned in 1974 from the Church of South India to his native England after a lifetime of absence, he was gripped with the realization that western society had become one of the world's great mission fields.[1] Since then, new movements for the evangelization of the West have sprung up everywhere, notable among them the "missional church" project and the identification of the "emerging church" as the hope for western Christianity.[2] Embedded in these movements is the conviction that western Christendom is dying and that a new missionary (or missional) groundswell is either emerging or waiting to be born.

Some are convinced that western mission boards are themselves dying vestiges of colonialism. In this view, we must stop sending missionaries in anything like the traditional way and begin a new life of corporate missional existence in our own backyards, networking with brothers and sisters in other nations as God leads us.

Perhaps this is God's way—time will tell as we trust the lead-

ing of the Holy Spirit. Whatever the future verdicts on our generation, I am convinced that Christian mission is never either/or—
either global or local. It is always both/and. There is more to be cel-
ebrated in the evangelical missionary movement since 1727, when
the Moravian Brethren movement began, than there is to be
decried.

For sure, whatever our convictions about western missions
and the re-evangelization of the west, we know our goals cannot
be reached without personal and corporate renewal. They are
quite unattainable unless God moves among us in both life-
changing and grace-filled ways.

The vision is simple. We know it well.

First, we can know God only through Jesus Christ.

Second, God loves the world. God's mission has always
focused on the unredeemed world. We joined a movement.

It is true, of course, that God also loves the church. The
church is his body, a covenant community of wholeness, of
shalom. But as missiologist Ralph Winter said, "Unless and until,
in faith, the future of the world becomes more important than the
future of the church, the church has no future."[3] The church is
always in danger of forgetting that God loves the world.

Third, Jesus invites us, even commands us, to take this good
news to every part of the world until he comes.

Fourth, he has promised to fill us with his Holy Spirit. We
are not alone.

Fifth, we will suffer as we go, just as Christ suffered for us.
We will go at the cost of our ambitions, our security, and our rep-
utations.

Finally, the vision is for the whole body, not just for a part.
But we cannot hold to any of this merely as a pleasant, comfort-
able pastime. It is either being lived out in lives of costly discipleship or it is the worst kind of word game. As Dietrich Bonhoeffer
once said, when Jesus calls a person, he calls that person to come
and die.

The vision is for mission:

- A mission initiated in prayer, bathed in prayer, consummated in prayer
- A mission that responds to God's initiative and holds fast to the centrality of Jesus, the authority of Scripture, and the anointing of the Holy Spirit
- A mission that takes seriously the judgment of God, in the hereafter as well as the here and now
- A mission that knows that suffering love is at the heart of the evangel and even embraces martyrdom as a way of witness
- A mission that forsakes the deed/word polarities found among too many Christians and rather is caught up in a New Testament worldview that does not recognize such a distinction
- A mission that does not focus on success and failure in terms of numbers, of worldwide denominational linkages, or of tradition
- A mission that is focused on the formation and nurture of new faith communities centered on Jesus, empowered by the Holy Spirit, and radical in obedience
- A mission that depends on the power of the Holy Spirit
- A mission that takes seriously the presence and partnership of the churches of the global south by radically reviewing, and asking God to transform, our systems of control and disposition
- A mission that is grass-roots—in the finest sense of that term. Such a mission avoids a creeping professionalism that sometimes substitutes "excellence" for faithfulness and excludes ordinary Christians

It is the mission of Jesus.

Vision Alone Is Not the Answer

We live in a society inundated with vision. Visionaries are lauded, whether in politics, business, or religion. Every organization worth its salt needs an up-to-date vision statement, words that capture the essence of what it is, along with the compelling aspirations that will ensure success and prominence in its realm and motivate its members to excellence.

Leaders are judged on the basis of their vision. To be known as a man or woman of vision is to have already achieved a significant level of success. Never mind the content of the vision or how fully it is realized.

Even local congregations are now urged to define their vision and mission in short statements that grip the imagination and give focus to the energy of the members. Furthermore, individuals are encouraged to develop their own personal mission and vision statements in the quest for excellence.

Vision has its place, no doubt.

The "Anabaptist vision," for example, has helped give shape to evangelical identity ever since such scholars as George H. Williams, Franklin Littell, and John Howard Yoder recast it in the twentieth century.[4] In other arenas, the visions of Sam Walton or Walt Disney are well known for the impact they have had on consumerism and entertainment in our culture. The vision of Martin Luther King Jr. electrified and changed an entire nation.

Yet in the end, vision alone is not the answer.

It is not the vision, but the substance, that makes the difference. Is it true? Is it worthy? Is it real? Is it lived? When it is lived, what is its effect? Is it lived with integrity? Is it a way of life?

It is easy to drift into thinking that a vision held intellectually is equivalent to a vision lived, that a vision stated is a vision realized. Perhaps that's why Jesus said so much about obedience. "Not everyone who says to me, 'Lord, Lord,' will enter the kingdom of heaven, but only the one who does the will of my Father in heaven" (Matthew 7:21 NRSV).

Was Jesus a man of vision? Somehow the phrase doesn't quite fit. A man of purpose, yes. A man of single-minded obedience, yes. Yet though his vision was crystal clear, it was not his vision but his life that made all the difference.

The way of reconciliation and peace in global mission is like that. It is, to be sure, a vision. But more than that, it is a path, a grace-filled life lived in dependence on God.

One life lived in fellowship with God is worth a thousand visions.

PASSION FOR JESUS, COMPASSION FOR THE WORLD

About AD 30, Jesus of Nazareth died on a Roman cross outside the city walls of Jerusalem. Three days later, God raised him from the dead. A few days later still, he ascended to heaven, and from there he poured out the Holy Spirit on a little group of his disciples.

The world has never been the same.

Empires rise and fall, but now, at the beginning of the third millennium from his birth, every human accomplishment is ultimately measured against his person. The light of his presence eclipses all other personal "lights" in human history. Abraham, Alexander, Caesar Augustus, Attila, Kublai Khan, Elizabeth I, Einstein, Gandhi—all pale in comparison.

Only a few other religious leaders—Moses, the Buddha, Muhammad—might bear some comparison, and they only by pointing away from themselves to the divine. Only Jesus could say, "And I, when I am lifted up from the earth, will draw all people to myself" (John 12:32 NRSV). Others who have made such awesome claims about their own persons have been closely and cynically watched by their generations, then quickly forgotten.

To the contrary, in his own and every generation since, Jesus has not been forgotten. Rather, he has been worshipped as the saving one, the transforming one. His followers circle the globe, singing the joy of knowing him.

While he was with his first disciples, he told them to go introduce him to every people group, every "nation," in the world. That's what Christian "mission" is all about.

Without Jesus, the world is lost, adrift on the sea of its own designs and resources. In Jesus, we have the very presence of God—redeeming, restoring, releasing.

What then is a "mission society"? It is simply a few of Jesus' followers, his redeemed and transformed ones, hearing his voice and obeying him. It is a little group of brothers and sisters joining millions of others in singing and living to the glory of the risen one—sending and going.

So we go to the world—here and everywhere he leads us. We are not essentially organizations, though we appear to be. Rather, we are ragtag groups of Jesus people.

Passion for Jesus expresses itself inevitably in compassion for the world. True compassion, of course, has little to do with merely getting enough material wealth to share with others. Of course, we'll share what we have of that. Instead, true compassion has everything to do with having Jesus' heart for the world.

After that, our hearts and our lives, all that we have and all that we are, are broken like bread for those who hunger. They too will see and feast and live.

Passion for Jesus, compassion for the world.

THE GLOBAL CHRISTIAN MOVEMENT

"Therefore go and make disciples of all nations, baptizing them in the name of the Father and of the Son and of the Holy Spirit, and teaching them to obey everything I have commanded you. And surely I am with you always, to the very end of the age" (Matthew 28:19-20).

These were Jesus' last instructions to us, his disciples. A few days later he ascended, and then there was Pentecost. After Pentecost, the New Testament takes up the thread with the stories of Peter and Paul, but drops it abruptly at the end of the book of Acts. There are a few further hints of how the story continued in some of the apostolic letters, but fewer than seventy years after Jesus was crucified, no more of the New Testament was written.

What happened next? Did the early church descend rapidly into apostasy, with no more missionary activity for fifteen hundred years? Did the vision die with the apostles and their immediate successors?

Thank God, no.

In fact, the early church spread with such zeal and effectiveness that, despite bloody persecutions, whole nations and even empires were impacted. The story of the Roman Empire is best known. Within fewer than three hundred years after Jesus died, the Christian witness had grown so strong throughout the empire that the emperor Constantine paved the way for Christianity to become the official state religion, a move that gradually weakened the faith in and around Rome more than the persecutions ever had.

But the Roman Empire was just one of many political entities. To the east of that empire lay another, the Persian, and Christianity spread rapidly throughout that region as well, becoming in time "the Church of the East." Even today the Christians of South India, beyond the old Persian Empire, recount how the apostle Thomas brought them the good news before he was martyred near Madras. Across Central Asia and on into China early Syrian and Persian missionaries took the good news to the Turkish tribes and the Han Chinese.

To the south lay Africa, and early Christian evangelists also took the gospel to the headwaters of the Nile, in what is today called Ethiopia. The modern Coptic Orthodox church there is surely one of the oldest in the world.

To the far northwest the witness spread into parts of what we now call the British Isles, spawning a powerful missionary movement among the Celtic tribes there. That movement continued for centuries and led eventually to the evangelization of European tribes on the continent. Many ancestors of modern German Christians heard the good news first from the lips of these flaming Celtic heralds.

Through the centuries since Pentecost, this passionate, Christ-centered witness has persisted—sometimes distorted by nationalistic or imperial powers, sometimes resisted with such ferocity that the ground was soaked with the blood of faithful martyrs, but never snuffed out. Largely because Christians are "not of this world," only a tiny fraction of the history of this global movement can be documented today, but the traces of it can be found in every part of the world.

The Waldensians of the thirteenth century, for example, translated and memorized Scripture in the contemporary languages of southern Europe, then traveled in pairs, teaching and preaching. Their message was simple, biblical, and Christ-centered.

Were they thanked? Yes, certainly by those who heard them gladly. But by the authorities they were burned at the stake, and their precious manuscripts burned with them. So ruthless were their enemies that very little of their work can be documented, yet it is known that they evangelized so zealously that perhaps half the population of southern Europe heard the good news from their lips, and many responded.

Sadly, once churches became "official" and state-sponsored, they often attempted to smother expressions of the faith that were more lively, more vital, and often more biblical. Yet in these official churches too, renewal movements abounded, so much so that one can never quite predict what the Spirit of God will do next. For example, there are powerful renewal movements today in the traditional Coptic churches of both Egypt and Ethiopia, touching the lives of thousands. In Ethiopia these on-fire Coptic Christians are called "Ortho-Pente." In other places one finds disciples of Jesus embedded so deeply in the cultures of other major world religions that they may be called Muslim, Hindu, or Jewish followers of Jesus. These are sometimes called "insider movements."

So one can explore all of world history since Pentecost and find fascinating glimpses of the spread of Christianity—a moving saga of transformed lives and changed peoples in every century. But how should we understand our own relationship to this whole? Are contemporary western believers churches somehow connected to this thrilling movement of the Spirit of God?

Yes, by all means.

For example, the Anabaptist movement in Europe after 1500, a movement to which many North American evangelicals can trace our historical and theological roots, was itself a missionary movement. Furthermore, those faithful believers helped blaze the trail for the modern evangelical missionary movement.

It happened something like this.

European Christianity in 1500 was pretty cold. Ruthless suppression by the authorities of renewal or evangelistic groups like the Waldensians had been all too effective. To the west, over in England, a spiritual fire had flamed for a time through the translation and preaching of John Wycliffe, and across to the east John Hus had preached a great revival in Bohemia. But Hus had been executed, and Wycliffe's bones were dug up and burned; there didn't seem to be much left except the smoldering ashes.

But then came Martin Luther with his bold proclamations of 1517, and within a decade all of Europe was seething with a new spiritual ferment. The "protestant" churches, excommunicated from Roman Catholicism, began to develop national or regional state churches of their own, and in the middle of all this sprang up groups of grass-roots, evangelical, radical Christians who gradually became known as "Anabaptists" because they rebaptized adults who had been baptized into the state churches as babies. In doing so they laid important spiritual foundations for the contemporary global evangelical and Pentecostal movements.

Actually, these brothers and sisters were simply behaving a lot like the Christians described on the pages of the New Testament and like many others who had gone before them—preaching the good news first to anyone who would listen to them in their own cultures, then spilling over into neighboring people groups or traveling long distances to share with parts of the world that had not yet heard. As far as they were concerned, they were simply normal Christians, so their name for each other was just "brothers."

Furthermore, like so many of those from earlier centuries, they were also opposed as heretics, fanatics, disturbers of the peace. So before long, they were also imprisoned, burned at the stake, and in some places hunted like wild animals. They hoped to go to the Ottoman Turks, the enemies of Europe to the east, and to the red men of the New World, but their vision was not to be fulfilled in their day.

Their persecution was so intense that before a century had

passed they had been hounded into the desolate and remote places of Europe or had begun to capitulate to the pressure.

Two hundred years later, though, in August 1727, a new revival broke out among some descendants of these radical European Christians. The location was Herrnhut, Germany, and the missionary movement that resulted was named "Moravian." Within a decade they had begun scattering around the world, making disciples.

One of the most notable of these was an Anglican priest named John Wesley, who encountered their powerful witness in January 1736, less than ten years later, as he traveled by ship to the colony of Georgia in the New World. A group of Moravian missionaries was traveling on his ship. When a fearsome Atlantic storm blew up, the third in a row, Wesley saw their faith in action as they continued with a worship service they had begun.

On January 25 he wrote in his journal:

> In the midst of the psalm wherewith their service began, the sea broke over, split the mainsail in pieces, covered the ship, and poured in between the decks, as if the great deep had already swallowed us up. A terrible screaming began among the English. The Germans [Moravian Christians] calmly sang on. I asked one of them afterward, "Were you not afraid?" He answered, "I thank God, no." I asked, "But were not your women and children afraid?" He replied, mildly, "No; our women and children are not afraid to die."[5]

Wesley was deeply moved by this testimony of faith, and he later found peace with Christ through their continuing witness, after which he spent two months being discipled at their center in Herrnhut, Germany. He in turn was used of God, along with others, to turn England back to God. In the next fifty years he logged 250,000 miles by horseback, preaching salvation by faith in Christ.

Within a year after Wesley died in 1791, an English Baptist

shoemaker named William Carey, also deeply influenced by the Moravian missionaries, sparked the beginning of the great century of missions (1792-1900) by writing a pamphlet entitled "An Enquiry into the Obligation of Christians to Use Means for the Conversion of the Heathens." In 1793, he sailed for India, where he spent the rest of his life as a missionary. He is recognized today as the "father of Protestant missions."

What does all this have to do with the twenty-first century? Simply this, that the radical Christians of medieval and Reformation Europe were used by God to help reconstruct the foundations of the New Testament "believers church" in European Christianity through their fearless testimony, despite the storm of persecution unleashed against them. Like many before them, they preached the simple biblical truth that the church consists of those who place their faith in Jesus as Savior and Lord, that we are made new creatures in Christ, that the church is a holy community of believers, that discipleship is not coerced, and that we are privileged to take this good news to the world.

As a result, their spiritual descendants have been used of God for nearly three hundred years in a global missions movement that has completely redrawn the "Christian map." At the beginning of the twenty-first century, three-quarters of the world's evangelical Christians lived in Latin America, Africa, and Asia. In contrast, as recently as 1950, more than that percentage had lived in Europe and North America. Thus these early European radicals were used of God to sow spiritual seed that has yielded a marvelous global missionary harvest.

Of course, this is not the only seed that has germinated and sprung up. No one group is the spiritual fountainhead of modern western Christianity. For example, devoted Roman Catholic missionaries also circled the globe with their witness in the sixteenth and seventeenth centuries, before the time of the Moravians and Wesley, laying the foundations of the global reach and numerical preponderance of the Roman Catholic Church today.

So those European believers-church radicals, who led many back to Christ in the sixteenth century, are simply one company in a great train of faithful saints stretching back to Pentecost. However, despite their apparent failure in their own time, "the blood of the martyrs is indeed the seed of the church," and this European witness was eventually fruitful beyond the experience of many Christians at other times.

So what?

As western Christians, let's reclaim our evangelistic and missionary heritage. It's at the core of the New Testament; it's also at the core of the sixteenth-century movements to which European Christians, whether Catholic or Protestant, trace our more recent roots. For too long we have emphasized our denominational or confessional distinctives without simultaneously focusing on that dynamic evangelistic center. Without this, every attempt to understand either the New Testament or European Christianity will fail, no matter how painstaking the scholarship. Jesus' last recorded words were "in Jerusalem, and in all Judea and Samaria, and to the ends of the earth" (Acts 1:8). The Anabaptists, for example, quoted the Great Commission more than any other Scripture when they appeared in court.

Furthermore, let's acknowledge with gratitude how broadly the global Christian church of the twenty-first century has embraced this simple evangelical biblicism. By God's grace, we have had some part to play in that. What a joy.

Finally, let's fling ourselves at the feet of Jesus in true communion and discipleship in our generation, abandoning ourselves once again to the Lord who bought us. There's no greater privilege, no nobler passion.

PART 2

THE PEOPLE

MISSIONARIES AND THEIR CHILDREN

We send all kinds of people cross-culturally in mission. Young, old, middle-aged; professionals, tradespeople, farmers, keepers at home; formally educated, informally educated; married, single, women, men; skilled, unskilled. Some support themselves as they go; most are supported by the regular gifts of congregations who send them.

We do observe that, after awhile, both missionaries and their children are notorious for being unable to "fit in" back home. One hears horror stories about how they just never make it. Their clothes, hairstyles, and cars—not to mention their strange values and personalities—draw knowing smiles or sympathetic shakes of the head.

Simultaneously, though, they carry a reputation for adaptability. Those "third-culture kids" can make themselves at home anywhere in the world within two weeks—making friends, affirming the new surroundings, and contributing with confidence.

Which of these stereotypes is true?

The answer, of course, is both. Almost ironically, the very gift of adaptability inherent in persons who have come to be at home in more than one culture makes it particularly difficult for them to be fully at home in any. For this reason the person who has lived in eastern Africa for even a few years is always, it seems, on the verge of going back. Why? Because that has now become one of his or her homes.

A missionary, in the classic sense, is simply one who has become bicultural for the sake of representing Jesus in another culture. Their children get a double dose of what missionary parents had. The parents had grown up in one cultural home. They were rooted in a particular "tribe." But their children know only the duality. They constantly flow back and forth between two cultures.

What do *they* do as adults? Where do they root?

Some of them never quite do. Those are the tragic, heart-wrenching stories of tortured souls who ask "who am I?" with crescendo—the echoes bouncing off brazen skies until the end. Of course, the children of missionaries are not the only ones who relentlessly hurl the identity question. But for those others who do, one often discovers in their histories the agony of a person who stood astride some cultural chasm.

But most find a place, a home. Many do what their parents did—and love it. Third-culture kids can make some of the best missionaries, identifying deeply with the new people groups to which they go. One meets them the world over—second-, third-, and fourth-generation missionary kids crossing cultures for the love of Christ.

Others are mission advocates in their home cultures. At our mission board, for example, almost all the members of the leadership team are either missionaries or their children. Evangelical congregations across the United States have dozens of such leaders advocating for international missions, even while they serve effectively in other arenas of service.

Missionaries and their children. Deprived, yes, but also profoundly gifted. At home almost everywhere, yet never quite. We send them and bless them.

Young Adults in Mission: The New Wave

I watched them from a distance, sometimes wishing I were younger. I knew they were spanning the globe, traveling in teams and trusting God to supply their needs. I knew they were praying, witnessing, serving. I knew their lives were being transformed by what they saw and experienced.

They were a new wave of young adults in mission, gradually making their way into the corporate consciousness of the North American evangelical churches in the 1970s. They were at first linked to such organizations as Operation Mobilization (OM) and Youth With a Mission (YWAM). But as time passed they appeared under all kinds of names from many different places.

I once encountered a large, winsome group of high-schoolers en route from Europe to the United States, clad in boots and warm in faith and joy, impacting the whole airplane with their free spirits. Upon inquiry, I learned that they were with Teen Missions.

There was another occasion when a group of thirteen showed up on our doorstep in the Middle East, one of the leaders looking for an old friend from preconversion days, one with whom she wanted to share her newfound faith in Christ—only to discover that her friend, who was living with us, had also met Jesus in the interim. It was a YWAM prayer team, and we spent an unforgettable evening introducing each other to what God was doing in our countries. There was a Christian from our denomination on the team as well, a team that had found us quite "by accident."

With the birthing of YES (Youth Evangelism Service) in the early 1980s, the movement came closer to home for North American Mennonites. We were now joining teams and also creating them. Eastern Pennsylvania leaders embraced and envisioned the movement in Anabaptist form and content, defending it staunchly against its critics.

What is the core of the new wave? Is it the centrality of discipleship training? Is it the principle of immediate practical application of what is learned in the classroom? Is it the team structure, reminiscent of the centuries-old Waldensian and Franciscan missionary patterns? Is it the throwing of oneself into situations where "faith is possible," learning dependence on God? Is it the connection between discipleship and mission, a connection that had flung the Celtic *peregrini* from their lonely islands into the forests of Europe to be flaming heralds for Jesus in the early Christian centuries?

Yes, all of this is somewhere near the core.

But perhaps there is something even more fundamental. Might this be a divine mobilization, spanning the globe as we wind toward an immense global harvest? Might this new wave of young adults in mission represent something quite beyond any program, be it YWAM, OM, YES, or RAD? Might there be an intrinsic spiritual connection between these western movements and those simultaneously sweeping through countries like China, Korea, Indonesia, Ethiopia, Brazil, and Argentina? Might the western movement of which we are a part be a weaker counterpart of something happening with even more radical effectiveness in other parts of the world?

There are stories, for example, of young Sudanese Christians who pile in teams onto the tops of loaded lorries and ride for many miles to distant Muslim villages in their own country. Then they stand in the marketplaces and preach the good news at great risk to their lives. They may well swap stories one day with western teams. For now, we know little about them, or they about us.

In the spring of 1995, at the Global Consultation on World Evangelization, I saw seventy thousand Korean youth in the Olympic stadium in Seoul committing their lives to the global harvest. Other similar rallies have taken place since then in different parts of the world. Of all this we receive only occasional glimpses.

God alone knows the deeper connections.

In any case, we know we are part of one global movement of grace, birthed and sustained in the heart of God. For the future, we see greater interconnections between what is happening there and here. Requests are pouring in from churches around the world to walk together in the formation of new discipleship training and mission centers for young adults. The Global Discipleship Training Alliance has been formed to stimulate their multiplication.[6] There are many other training and networking ventures of all kinds.

We know we have much to learn from them. We are far from complete in ourselves. Numerical growth in overseas sister churches exceeds ours in North America. Greater humility is needed for western church and mission, greater eagerness to sit at the feet of Jesus as he serves us through them.

We know that what has been birthed in this new wave of young adults in mission is still in its adolescence. But we tremble with anticipation of what it may mean when full-grown. We rejoice at the tens of thousands of young adults who have been trained in YWAM and its sister programs. We see a new generation of pioneer witnesses being born to maturity.

We know that the seeds of radical discipleship are here—not simply on the basis of our rootage in powerful movements of the

Spirit at other times in other places, but on the basis of contemporary encounters with the risen Christ, both in the training centers and in the far-flung corners of the world to which they go. We see the need for further foundation building and discipling to go on to the next stages of long-term, pioneer teaming along the frontiers. We are praying and planning.

We know, and we see. We tremble, and we rejoice. All is ours, for we belong to Christ, and Christ to God. The new wave of young adults in mission is indeed a global movement birthed in the heart of God.

DEVELOPING HEARTS FOR MISSIONS

What leads a person to missions? Why do some children grow up to be world Christians, and others do not?

Concerned Christian parents, especially, discuss such questions frequently, looking for clues. Is it the right school, the right church? Is it maintaining the right relationships with our children? Is it all the grace of God?

The answers are as complex as we are. Yet there are a few simple guidelines that, when followed, make a world of difference.

The most important role of Christian parents, of course, is simply to introduce their children to Jesus. Every person either meets Jesus and is transformed, or makes critical life decisions apart from God. Children are not puppets. I can do everything else "right," but unless my children meet Jesus, they will never become world Christians. They may be religious, but they will not become winsome witnesses.

The passion to introduce others to Christ is born from what he is doing for me. If Jesus is not changing me, I will have little interest in introducing others to him. If I do not care about introducing people around me to Jesus, my spiritual concern for others around the world remains hypothetical or hypocritical. I may care about their physical well-being, but I will not really be concerned about their eternal destiny, because mine is in question.

It also goes without saying that children are more influenced by who their parents are than by what their parents say. Parents are teachers of their children, true. But the most effective teachers are doers—praying, giving, reaching out to those around them.

Children of such parents are powerfully shaped by their parents' lives. They may fail to meet Jesus themselves, but they will never forget how their parents lived, and they will always remember to whom they, like their parents, may turn. It is the God who came to us in Christ.

Finally, one of our most critical kingdom roles is discipling our children. We may disciple others, but if we fail to reach out to those who are closest to us, our children, we send an awful message: *Those out there are more important to me than you are.* None of us want to send that message, but sometimes we do, and the results are sobering.

There's much, much more, of course. Perhaps the hardest lesson we ever learn is that of sacrificial love. What does it mean to give up everything to follow Christ? Does it mean that we abandon our children?

No, a thousand times, no. But together with our children, we can say yes.

I remember the day our youngest son was weeping in the back seat of our car as we left home for a mission task to which we felt a deep sense of call but to which he did not want to accompany us. We stopped the car, and I asked Jewel to take the wheel. I crawled into the back seat with him, and together we wept as we went. There was pain, but there was also in-breaking joy. Years later when that same son preached his first sermon in another land, he began by telling that story and saying, "That's why I can preach in your language today."

ARE WE HOLISTIC?

Are we preaching the whole gospel for the whole world? Do we teach and live the whole gospel for a broken world? In short, are we holistic? That is, do we unite word and deed, evangelism and social justice, private and public faith in the mission to which God has called us?

Western Christians have been preoccupied with this question. Perhaps it is our guilty conscience. Lesslie Newbigin argued that modern western culture has driven a deep wedge between our private and our public worlds. Religion and all other "values" are private and subjective, whereas science and the world of "facts" are public and objective.[7] As a result, all religious expression is relativized and trivialized. Christians' preoccupation with holism, then, may be a powerful spiritual urge to shake off this ungodly dichotomy dictated by our culture.

Or perhaps it is a legacy of the theological split between fundamentalism and modernism in late nineteenth-century North American evangelicalism, in which the fundamentalists went for evangelism while the modernists went for social justice. That, at least, is one stereotype.

In either case, the question keeps occurring. Are we holistic? In our mission, do we care about both body and soul? Or is it just soul? Or just body?

It is clear that Jesus never tolerated such distinctions. His words and deeds of power were a seamless garment that was never rent. He taught, and he healed. He exposed the hypocrisy of both doers and sayers. What he taught, he lived. What he lived, he taught. What he lived and taught, he was.

I am encouraged by the holism of the western missionary community, whether short or long term. Through them, the Lord is raising up new churches, healing the sick, caring for the needy, developing businesses, addressing conflicts, making peace. In the modern western church, missionaries are, on the whole, the most holistic people I know.

The same was true in the ancient church. The Celtic monk and missionary Columban (543-615) once said, "He who says he believes in Christ ought to walk as Christ walked, poor and humble and always preaching the truth."[8] Bosch wrote, "The monks were poor, and they worked incredibly hard; they plowed, hedged, drained morasses, cleared away forests, did carpentry, thatched, and built roads and bridges."

Contemporary missionaries walk in such a train. By the grace of God, we long to be holistic—walking, serving, and preaching like Jesus in the power of the Spirit. This is our vision, and that of the churches we represent.

We believe it is the vision of Jesus for all his people. May our culture never take us captive.

WANT A NEW WORLDVIEW?

Counterintuitive choices are the backbone of discovery.

Want to find a good wife? Stop looking, and focus on being who God wants you to be. Want to make money dairy farming? Treat your cows (and incidentally, yourself) right by dividing your farm up into dozens of little pastures and let them feed themselves by intensive grazing. Want to rest? Walk. Want a fulfilling retirement? Work. Want to find the Far East? Sail west!

Want a new worldview? Read the Bible.

Read the Bible? "Well, yes," you say, "I read the Bible from time to time—but not to get a new worldview. I read the Bible for inspiration, for advice on how to live, for eternal spiritual truths. God speaks to me through the Bible. But read the Bible for a new worldview? I don't think so."

Too rare, indeed, is the Christian who reads the Bible for a new worldview. Yet that is the heart and soul of conversion.

Some people look, for example, at "the problem of evil." Westerners have wrestled with it for centuries. If God is both sovereign and good, we ask, how can he allow evil to triumph, or even to exist? For that matter, how can God's sovereignty and human free will exist simultaneously? Or if God is sovereign, is not everything that happens his will? Why do bad things happen to good people?

Evil and God. God and evil. What a tragedy.

In ways such as these the God of the Bible gets associated with or even blamed for evil. Yet in contrast the Bible introduces us to the only One who has both the will and the power to deliver us from evil. To be converted is to see the world the way he does and to walk in that peace and power.

He sees our enemy Satan along with the spiritual forces that seek to destroy us. He sees our own awful pride and rebellion. But he also sees the one he sent, our redeemer, the Lamb of God. He sees and understands the spiritual battle in which we are engaged, and he gives us power to overcome. Instead of a "problem," victory.

This is a "warfare worldview."[9] It stands in sharp contrast to the humanistic materialism of western culture. It also counters the benign, inoffensive deism of much of popular Christianity.

A new worldview from reading an ancient book? Indeed. Counterintuitive perhaps, but revolutionary for sure.

And what joy in the discovery. Mission is nothing less than the living of that joy.

AGAINST THE TIDE

There are those who would rob us. There are those who would tell us that our ancestors died in vain, that the simple obedience of faith in Jesus is old-fashioned and passé, that to read the Bible and take it seriously is naive. There are those who would tout the new because it is new and smile away the old merely because it is old.

Refuse to be conned! The church of Jesus Christ is here today because there have been men and women in every generation who have gone against the tide. Ours is no exception.

There is, of course, something to be said for fitting in, for "identifying," for adapting. Missionaries often lead that charge. But *contextualization* is a buzzword that can kill as well as give life. And fitting in begs the question: fitting into what?

When Jesus said, "Take up your cross," it was death to adapting. And when he said, "The world will hate you," he did not mean that we would be hated because we fit in so well.

So, what does it mean to go against the tide? Is it stubbornness, peculiarity, or lambasting the culture into which one happens to be born? Is it cynicism, tough-minded analysis, or radical social action? Hardly.

Jesus was clearly not saying, "Follow me, and I will make you a crackpot." Rather, he was saying, "Be aligned with God."

Alignment with God is the most natural thing in the world.

It is actually the ultimate form of fitting in. Yet because so few are willing to be so aligned, those few inevitably appear odd, strange, naive, or downright dangerous to the unaligned world. They are going against the tide.

Since mission is all about alignment with God, it will then normally be out of step with its world. Missionaries will be out of step with the societies *from* which they go, and they'll be out of step with the cultures *to* which they go.

Poor people, doomed to be "strangers and pilgrims" whether at home or abroad. Blessed people, realigned.

LEADERSHIP

What does leadership have to do with love? At first thought, perhaps almost nothing. The words most often used to describe effective leadership in our society are *vision, challenge, inspiration, enabling, modeling, encouraging, strategic thinking, planning, deciding, delegating, empowering, mentoring, courage, boldness, teamwork, listening,* and *servanthood.*

Whether in politics, business, education, or the church, these words and others like them fly thick and fast whenever leadership is discussed. And indeed leadership is *often* discussed.

Love, however, is strikingly absent from the list. Perhaps it's assumed to underlie all the other characteristics of good leadership. Perhaps it's too sentimental, too linked to sexual union. Perhaps it seems wimpy or weak to talk of love. Perhaps we think it a good descriptive word for followers but not for leaders.

In any case, love may be a good theological, moral, or marriage-and-family concept. But it rarely turns up in discussions of leadership, even among Christians.

Yet it should.

For love is the bedrock of all true leadership. A leader who does not love may do a thousand things right, but the absence of love dooms all else to tawdry insignificance.

Jesus said it best: the great commands are love of God and love of neighbor (see Matthew 22:37-40). Furthermore, everyone will know that we are his disciples if we love each other (see John 13:35).

Someone asks, "But what do these universal commands have to do with *leadership*? These are for everyone, not particularly for the leader. The truly effective leader, in order to be a leader, must focus significant energy elsewhere, even while obeying the universal injunction to love."

No! That's precisely our problem. To the contrary, leadership has everything to do with love. The real authority to lead springs directly from lives laid down in willing service for others. Effective leadership is not coercive or manipulative; rather, it is God-centered, sacrificial love in the pattern of Jesus.

This love, of course, is not merely a feeling or emotion. It is, in fact, a thoroughly left-brained, even scientific, will for the good of the other. It is a decision, a life-long no to self and yes to the One who created us. It is also the poetry of a life dedicated to the beauty of divine creativity expressed in everyone we meet.

Such lovers become leaders. Such leaders, in turn, are loved. Yes, like Jesus they are also spurned. Yet they *lead*. For though they die, they rise again. Indeed, we need a new word in our leadership vocabulary. *Love*.

Neither Born Nor Self-Made

What makes a Christian witness "successful"?

There's the well-worn adage that leaders are born, not made. It's nature, not nurture. Either one is born with the genes for achievement or not. If not, we might as well not waste the effort trying.

On the other hand, American how-to pop culture is full of the complementary assumption that leaders are self-made. How to get wealth, lose weight, achieve all sorts of other goals—in general, how to become who we want to be. We live in a virtual paradise of individual achievement, making the most of whatever genes we were born with.

But maybe it's a fool's paradise. Not because we lack the right genetic codes for achievement and not because there's nothing we can do to improve ourselves—but maybe, just maybe, in our zeal for self-improvement we have missed another essential ingredient.

That is, we become successful because *others* choose to make us so.

Immediately we shy away. The personal independence so highly valued in our culture is affronted. My success dependent on others? Never. It's whatever equipment I was born with, coupled with lots of elbow grease.

Yet a moment's reflection corrects the illusion. Parents do, after all, make a world of difference in what children become. Schools make a difference. So do societies.

Or in other words, how *I* relate to others makes a difference in what *they* are able to become. A significant difference. And with that realization comes an awesome awareness. I may choose either success or failure for many about me.

In fact, Christian mission is born out of that awareness. So too is discipling the brother or sister. Missions and discipling, if authentic, are based on a deep desire for the success of the other person. God's marvelous gift of eternal life, in all its dimensions, is for *everyone*.

Every time I forgive, I contribute to the success of another. Every time I encourage, pray, bless, confront in love, serve, hold my tongue, rejoice, share important information, listen, mentor, learn . . .

On the other hand, every time I cherish resentment, seek my own way, envy, criticize, or use another for my selfish ends, I contribute to their failure.

As a result, the world is full of broken lives, dashed dreams, unfulfilled longings. And even if all my dreams were to be met and those of friends and neighbors about me dashed to the ground, my life would not be a success at all. Rather, it would be a great failure to reach out in the love of Jesus.

'I Almost Lost My Faith'

A woman of God, now nearing middle age, was reflecting on her youth. She told me how she went off to school in a place known for defending the faith, for producing missionaries, for being a safe place to sink one's roots deep into the Word of God, for providing a setting in which lives are transformed.

Enjoying the conversation, I was inwardly gearing up for another vibrant testimony of how one more person met Jesus there. All my stereotypes were humming smoothly. Then came the shock.

"I almost lost my faith there," she said.

Now I was all ears. Did she fall in with the wrong crowd? Was her roommate some rebellious daughter sent by her parents in vain hope of a heart change? Did some highly esteemed teacher or classmate disappoint her?

"No, it wasn't that," she said. "It was just that everything was so intellectual. We had to have reasons for everything, to find our way to the truth through all the arguments. It somehow seemed impossible, having learned to know God, just to build on that solid foundation with simple faith, learning to know him better and better."

As she spoke, my long-held assumptions began to shake. After all, this was one place where the truth was defended at every turn, where students were sheltered and left school having grown in faith. Spiritual stalwarts walked the halls. This was a place about which I could confidently say, "Go and meet Jesus there."

Then I thought she must have attended that school when it was at some low point. So I asked when it was that she had attended.

Again came an unexpected answer. She named the years, and I was dumbfounded, for those were high-water years. Classrooms were packed; teachers were on fire; students prayed half the night.

Sobered, I knew in those moments that God had opened another window in my understanding. I saw that these very training programs established for a godly purpose could have hidden and opposite effects from what was intended. I saw that the effect in one life would not necessarily be replicated in another. I looked into the face of a passionate, joyous sister in Christ who nevertheless had not been encouraged in her journey of faith in a place dedicated to that very encouragement.

To be sure, she did meet God there. But not, she said, before she almost lost her faith, almost died from friendly fire.

I saw the potential spiritual oppressiveness of the good systems we create. I saw the perils of human reason, even when we attempt to apply it for its highest purposes. I saw how fraught with imperfection are all our designs to bring glory to God. I saw something of how unique are the ways of God with each new person we meet.

I thanked God for another surprise along the way, and I was reminded that there are many more to come. Thank you too, Greta.

WHAT IS SUCCESS?

> Though thy name be spread abroad
> Like winged seed from shore to shore,
> What thou art before thy God—
> That thou art, and nothing more.

These old lines, appropriately anonymous, quaintly but pointedly qualify every human criterion for success. Though it is not wrong to succeed, we know that each success carries its own temptation to demonic distortion.

We know well the usual pitfalls, deceptive as they are. Reputation, wealth, and power are all accompanied by that inner nudge to place myself at the center, inviting misdirected worship: *See who I am. Be impressed by what I have done.*

But pride is equally likely to distort religious or spiritual "success." The very mission on which we are sent becomes ours instead of God's. We substitute appearance for reality, form for substance, death for life.

For decades, our mission board has frequently served as a channel to express the heart of God for new creation. This is not a new creation easily identified by various criteria of success as they are generally perceived. Rather, it is one expressed in weakness, vulnerability, and the peace and joy that are fruit of the Spirit.

Yet wherever this new creation appears, it too can be promoted as our success or our effectiveness in mission. God is robbed of his glory, and we camouflage the splendor of divine achievement by embracing it as our own.

Yet also just as surely as we do this, God turns to others who rejoice in him. Ultimate success, then, is simply to "be before our God."[10]

LEADING

Everyone wants to be a leader, but no one wants to lead. It's not that simple, of course. Yet the truth of that statement makes us uncomfortable. Why?

Perhaps it is because being a leader is a position of prestige, recognition, and authority. We like that. Simultaneously, however, true leading means risk, vulnerability, wounds, and selfless service. We don't like that so much.

One of the fringe benefits of Christian witness, especially when it is cross-cultural, is that the witness moves out of a fairly well-defined comfort zone onto someone else's turf. Whatever the formal attributes of being a leader one may have carried on one's own turf, these attributes instantly mean much less when we move to someone else's. Often they mean nothing at all.

But when one leads through vulnerability and selfless service, that kind of leading never gets stripped away, because it is not tied to recognition. Rather, it is tied to one's inmost being before God. So if the Christian witness is willing to be stripped of the outward, the inward only shines more brightly.

This kind of leading is so different from our normal concepts of leadership that we should probably find another word for it. Perhaps *serving* would do. But the problem is, we quickly transform the words like *servant* or *minister* into just "being a leader." For example, we refer to government ministers or ministers in the church. A person might, indeed, be a true leader in such positions. But the fewer who are, the more the very terms *serving* or *ministering* lose their essential meanings. For many, these essential meanings are long gone.

Shall we then ditch all forms of positional leadership in the church? Shall we reserve the term *leader* only for those outside the church who occupy positions of power? Should we stop giving leadership seminars or talking about "leadership development" in the body of Christ? Perhaps we should. . . .

But no. To be sure, true leading of risk, vulnerability, and selfless service is an important aspect of every disciple's walk with God. But we do not discount the peculiar splendor of the presence of Jesus when one who is called to be a leader in some position of authority also lives with the basin and towel—taking risks, facing danger, being vulnerable.

How do we empower such Christlike leaders? The obvious first answer is that we cannot. Only God can do that. But we can partner with God. We can pray. We can see where the Holy Spirit is being poured out on men and women of faith, and we can call them to lead.

In cross-cultural settings where new circles of churches are being called into existence, we as missionaries can step out of positions of leadership ourselves and give them to our new brothers and sisters. Yes, it's risky. Yes, there are dangers.

But the risk and the vulnerability, together with Christ, are full of promise.

IF I WERE YOUNG AGAIN

If I were a young Christian again, one of my two top priorities would be to go into short-term missions. I'd join a discipleship training program, become part of a team, and go.

Sure, I know there are lots of other options. I could hurry into a baccalaureate program, get a head start on the job market by learning a trade, or simply explore the world's options through travel.

As a young man, I did all that, and more. I was curious, eager to learn, and endlessly intrigued by all the options. I was an explorer, as I still am. But far and away, what I did that had the greatest transformative effect on the rest of my life were the steps I took in learning to know God and making him known.

I installed drywall before I was twenty, hurried through Eastern Mennonite University with two majors in three and a half years, and twice explored Europe—once on my own and once with Mennonite Central Committee behind the Iron Curtain. A little bit crazy, perhaps, though I'd probably do it again.

Yet at the center I was learning to know God and becoming a disciple of Jesus. I knew it then, and now I see it ten times over. In dozens of ways I was drawn into the heart of the Christian community—teaching summer Bible school in poverty-stricken communities; attending Rosedale Bible College; forming a covenanted collegiate group to pray, worship, and go; joining the new spiritual renewal movement beginning to burst out around the edges of the college community; helping create agricultural cooperatives in the heart of Mississippi.

Later, as a father of teenagers, I told my friends in Ohio, "We're either going to start a discipleship training program for young adults right here, or I'll send my children out there somewhere to find one." Together, we began the Reach program, using YES as one of our primary models. All my children are Reach alumni. They weren't forced to go, of course, but they knew without a doubt the heart of their father.

I know the critiques of short-term missions. They are expensive, more for the benefit of those who go than of those to whom they go, divert attention from long-term commitments, and they're even a burden for the people at their destinations. They're the last gasp of western colonial missions.

We take those critiques seriously, as we should. But we also know that short-term missions have always been a key gateway to lifetimes of service in the kingdom. They started with Jesus when he sent the twelve, then the seventy. They continued with Paul and Barnabas in their foray into Asia Minor. The Anabaptists sent their short-termers all over Europe. John Wesley was a short-termer (two months) with the Moravians on the continent before God set England spiritually ablaze through the long-term team Wesley led.

So we're totally unapologetic about short-term missions. So the whole world will know Jesus Christ as Lord.

EMPIRE AND MISSION

God is wonderfully creative in loving and reaching the world. We often rightly emphasize how God uses ordinary people in mission. "Little people" in "little places" seem to be his favorite plan.

But his creativity does not stop there. God also uses big movements, great nations—even empires.

For example, there was Rome, the great civilization of the Mediterranean basin. Two thousand years later, I have walked with awe on Roman roads, everywhere from the dusty plains of Jordan in the east to the hills of southern Wales in the west. One of the most remarkable was a winding stretch of Roman road on the mountains above Philippi in modern Greece, still almost as usable as the day those massive, flat stones were first laid.

Jesus, Peter, and Paul walked those roads in the midst of that empire. Western enthusiasts for Roman law and order have doubtless sometimes overemphasized the importance of the Roman Empire for the spread of the gospel, for we know that the good news quickly spread far beyond its reaches. Nevertheless, God used Rome in remarkable ways. Greek, the language of culture throughout the empire, coupled with efficient Roman administration, opened doors everywhere for the spread of the early church.

The same is true in our own time. The British and American empires of the western world have encircled the globe with their language, administrative systems, and technology. These empires, like that of Rome, have opened countless doors for the contemporary spread of the good news.

English teaching is one of these doors, created by the almost universal demand to learn English, the native tongue of these modern empires. As a result, Christian witnesses have fanned out around the world, using their skills in teaching English just as Paul used his as a tentmaker both as a breadwinning occupation and as a point of connection in communication.

I well remember the day after teaching a routine class in freshman English at a university in the Middle East, when I realized that the anointing of the Holy Spirit for that task was just as real as when I stood behind a pulpit in a Christian meetinghouse. The almost palpable sense of the Spirit's presence, the joy and freedom in sharing, the sense that those who heard were somehow being attracted to Jesus—it was all there.

I had gone to that city for the purpose of Christian witness just as certainly as Paul had gone to Ephesus. In both cases, the presence of empire had helped to open doors, and in both cases the Holy Spirit moved. What a gift to walk with God in the twenty-first century as Paul did in the first.

Does God depend on empire for reaching out to a needy world? Is the Roman road, colonialism, or English (or Greek) necessary for the spread of the gospel? Thank God, no. But does God use empire? You bet.

FINISHING WELL

It is an art to finish well. Not to relax into bland mediocrity with the end in view. Not to rest on one's laurels prematurely. Not to dally near the finish line. Not to presume.

The ancient king Ahab put it succinctly, "One who puts on his armor should not boast like one who takes it off" (1 Kings 20:11).

So we strive to finish well. Finish tasks, roles, races, positions, life itself. It's somehow easier to begin well than to finish well, so we focus, appropriately, on the finish.

Time was when most people had a vocation that enveloped a lifetime. A farmer was a farmer from beginning to end. So also pastors, teachers, doctors, builders, and missionaries. And many still live such lifetimes. One calling, one focus, one finish.

But the world has changed. With growing cultural complexity and specialization, the art of finishing may be employed repeatedly in a single lifetime. I have a friend who started adult life as a medical doctor but now works as a lawyer. You doubtless have those friends too.

Among all the rest, there is a very special group of "finishers" in Christian mission. They are people who, usually after age forty-five, leave the occupations they have pursued to spend their later years in mission. They are no longer responsible for the care of young children, and they have freedom to finish their active lives along the frontiers of cross-cultural witness and service.

In one sense they are beginners, not finishers. They take bold steps of faith—learning new languages, adopting new cultures, daring to attempt what common wisdom has normally reserved for the young, healthy, and idealistic. You can't teach an old dog new tricks, after all.

But in spite of that common wisdom, these finishers often succeed and contribute beyond the expectations of both themselves and their younger peers. Yes, it's harder to learn a new language at fifty-five than at twenty-five. Yet one can still learn at fifty-five, and behind that learning stands a lifetime in the school of God. There is a wealth of transferable wisdom and insight that cuts across the whole human community and can be tapped from one culture to another.

So it is that a finisher who is a beginner can nevertheless be led of the Spirit in mission to finish once more in God-given splendor. A Beryl Forrester in the Gambia and Guinea-Bissau, like a Lesslie Newbigin back in his long-abandoned native England after having lived one lifetime in India, is indeed a priceless treasure.

So come, finishers. Come puncture the myth that cross-cultural mission is only an option for the children or grandchildren. Grandparents, hear the invitation. You're finishers, but far from finished. So the whole world will know Jesus Christ as Lord.

A SINGLE VISION

Keep the main thing the main thing. That's simple, but ever so hard to do. To begin with, there are temptations to pride, selfishness, lust, and greed. And the grosser temptations aside, there are also distractions of survival, injustice, laziness, and fear.

If all this were not enough, there are nobler aspirations of nation, clan, family, and self-care. In the end, we may conclude, the undistracted life is an impossible ideal. We'll do the best we can within whatever circumstances we live, and hope that is good enough.

But a single vision? Never.

Yet such fatalism does not behoove the child of God. There are resources in the Holy Spirit that take us far beyond our natural capacities—redeeming, transforming, empowering. Men and women of faith in every generation rise above the trammels of their times, living with a single vision, eyes fixed on Jesus.

One of God's special gifts to the world is the single woman or man who sets aside even the priorities of marriage to focus on the kingdom. Paul wrote eloquently of this gift to the Corinthian church: "An unmarried man is concerned about the Lord's affairs." The aim of the unmarried woman "is to be devoted to the Lord in both body and spirit." I want you, Paul wrote, to have "undivided devotion to the Lord" (1 Corinthians 7:32-35).

The European Protestant reformers reacted to some perceived excesses in the promotion of single life by the Catholic Church, and as a result we have experienced four hundred years of relative barrenness in the ministry of singles. Perhaps, though, we are on the verge of recapturing an ancient vision.

For example, John R. W. Stott, the anointed evangelical Anglican leader of the last generation, lived an enormously productive, focused life as a single man in Christ. Few persons in his generation had the global impact he did. Perhaps only Mother Teresa or Pope John Paul II, also both single, might be compared favorably. But they also stood in a long tradition of blessed singleness.

Thousands of others, less well known, could be named. I was nurtured and discipled by single women of God, Ruth Yoder and Mabel Maust, who gave their entire lives to ministry in Appalachia, each carrying a single vision that set hearts ablaze throughout the hills. One of the most radically faithful and fruitful Mennonite missionary men I have known, Dan Byler, has labored quietly in Nicaragua and southeast Asia, setting the standard for a whole generation to come.

Ponder it and compose your own list. They are everywhere. Whether everyone now single will serve for a whole lifetime without marriage is not the issue. But those who flame for God with single, passionate focus send a bright and fulsome message.

A single vision, a vision for singles. The two are not unrelated.

Part 3

The Walk

From Above? From Below?

Partnership! In mission circles, we hear about it, talk about it, everywhere. We partner with each other, partner with congregations, partner with other mission societies. We partner with overseas churches, partner with international mission groups, partner with the global Christian community. And of course we partner with God.

We all know how to wear out good words. Then every so often we also try to rescue an old, over-used word like *partnership*. We know the word is worn thin. We know that many other realities pose under the guise of partnership—realities like paternalism, arrogance, codependence, domination, selfishness. But we also believe that there is a partnership unmarred by any of those, a partnership born in heaven and given as gracious gift to those who receive.

It is a reality that leaps across the barriers of race, class, wealth, sex, education, and culture and affirms the unity of the Spirit of God. Though it recognizes differences where they exist, it refuses to major on those differences. Rather, it embraces brother and sister in love, looking constantly for ways to give, to receive, to venture and dare in common vision. We press on to discover new dimensions of that reality.

In 1800 no vestige of Christianity remained in most of sub-Saharan Africa; today, Africa is sometimes referred to as the

"Christian continent." We are challenged profoundly by the faith, witness, and love of millions of sisters and brothers there. What do we have to offer? What may we receive?

In 1950 a high percentage of cross-cultural Christian mission flowed from communities in North America and Europe. In the twenty-first century the tide has turned, and many of the most vital mission currents are flowing from communities in Latin America, Africa, and Asia. What may we receive? What do we have to offer? How may we venture and dare together—arms linked, vision clear, steps firm?

We are learning, step by step. We are learning that our wealth is sometimes less a gift than we had imagined, that the faith and prayer of our brothers and sisters often make ours seem paltry by comparison, but that nevertheless in God's grace we have something to share.

It is so easy to posture ourselves in mission "from above," in superiority of knowledge, wealth, technology, and power. But Jesus met us from below—in poverty, in weakness, in obscurity, in humility—even though he came from above.

Once again in our time we dare to dream and pray that such might be our gift as we reach out to partner in mission with our friends around the world, together moving from the foot of the cross.

'I Was in Prison'

I wonder how Jesus' description of the great separation at the end of the age might have been given by some of us (see Matthew 25:31-46).

I can imagine. "I was your neighbor, and you invited me to church. I was lost, and you spent thousands of dollars getting the good news onto the radio waves. I was a secular humanist, and you planted a church in my neighborhood. I lived in the 10/40 Window, and you came to preach to me.[11] Therefore, come you who are blessed by my Father, take your inheritance. . . ."

Or perhaps, "I was a lukewarm Protestant, and you explained the gospel of peace. I was a nationalistic God-and-country patriot, and you gave me a global perspective. I was a disgruntled post-Christian pagan, and you recommended a book on the Anabaptist vision. I was an individualistic westerner, and you introduced me to the faith community. Therefore, come you who are blessed. . . ."

I wonder. Jesus, by comparison, was shocking. "I was hungry and you gave me something to eat. I was thirsty and you gave me something to drink. I was a stranger and you invited me in. . . . I was sick. . . . I was in prison and you came to visit me."

Such scandalous simplicity! Such mundane concern for the other. Such dramatic disregard for religious formulations. Just a direct, unpretentious response to human need, and a mind-boggling identification of all such need as his need.

Just about the time I think I have Jesus figured out, he catches me totally off guard with something like "I was in prison." Incredible man.

It's downright frustrating. We get everything down to a science—evangelism, discipleship, community, church planting, renewal, care groups, missions, personal spiritual disciplines, hearing God, global Christianity, vision statements, cross-cultural sensitivity—then Jesus walks by and says, "I am in prison." Meddling, that's it. The doctorate is almost finished, the business is almost secure, we're ready to serve in a big way and he says, "I'm sick." It makes you feel like screaming.

But then the scenes flash to mind. Everywhere ordinary brothers and sisters, moved by the Spirit, are doing it. Feeding the hungry, taking in strangers, tending the sick, going to the prisons. The programs aren't flashy, the headlines don't carry the news, but Jesus incarnate in his people is reaching out to "the least of these."

Whether in Lancaster County, Philadelphia, the Deep South, or Cusco, Peru, Jesus is on the move.

DEFINING WITNESS

What is witness? Is it what we say or what we do? Is it both?

Evangelical Christians have written books, preached sermons, taught courses and in other ways spent countless hours trying to overcome a troubling polarity centered on these questions, which have crept into our lives and thought. In the end, all of us know that word and deed cannot be separated, that every word is a deed and every deed is a word, and that witness is somehow both. Yet the questions do not go away easily.

Even though we know that word and deed are a seamless garment that cannot be torn along some natural line, we come face to face with our fallen humanity each time a word is spoken but not echoed by deed, each time a deed is done but not complemented by the word of life. Something is missing. There is a hypocrisy, an incompleteness, of both word and deed. Though we affirm the unity, they are torn apart again and again in our experience, and we are troubled.

Is there a way through? Can we get beyond hypocrisy and incompleteness in witness? Yes, there is a way, one that is widely known but little traveled. It is the way of identification with Jesus.

Some signposts on the way:

Witness begins with what we see. Our preoccupation with word and deed is really a preoccupation with ourselves. What matters is not what we say or do, but what God has done.

Jesus is alive! God is living and speaking among us, changing lives. We are not purveyors of an ideology, a philosophy of life, or a lifestyle. Rather, Jesus met us on the road, delivered us from idolatry, and changed our lives forever. The focus of witness is not what we say or do, but God.

Witness is being. Again, a witness cannot be defined by either words or deeds, or both. A witness simply is. Some are witnesses; some are not. Those who have met Jesus and who have died and risen with him are witnesses. The old life of self-government is gone. Jesus is Lord! Furthermore, he lives within us. Old passions are being replaced by new. What we could never say or do, he does.

Witness is overflowing joy and service born out of death to the bondage of the old world and the rich release of eternal life. The old world doesn't understand the new, but it is being swallowed up by the new. The time is approaching when "the earth will be filled with the knowledge of the glory of the Lord, as the waters cover the sea" (Habakkuk 2:14).

This presence of God is manifested in joy unspeakable and full of glory. This is the authentic witness for which we yearn. Love that suffers, forgives, and overwhelms. Eternal life that flows and never stops—giving, giving, giving even in the face of hostility and misunderstanding. Joy that flows like a river.

Such witness is quite beyond us, whether in word or deed. But it's not beyond God, mightily at work within us by the Holy Spirit. This is the way of Jesus.

THE GREATEST MIRACLE

The story of missions is a story of miracles. Beginning with Abraham and continuing with Joseph, Moses, Naomi, Elijah, Jonah, Peter, and Paul, the Bible itself is full of the sagas of men and women on impossible journeys of faith in mission, journeys that succeeded against all odds.

The history of the Christian movement since Pentecost merely extends that record. Everywhere are the footprints of God—impossible visions fulfilled, breathtaking transformations of individuals, communities, and nations. It is a mountain that is slowly but surely filling the whole earth (see Daniel 2:35, 44).

And what is the greatest of all? It is without doubt the coming of Jesus. A birth unpreceded by human sexual intimacy, a life lived in unbroken intimacy with his Father and poured out in compassion for all he met, and a sacrificial death for all humanity. All this from a man who said, "Before Abraham was born, I am!" (John 8:58).

It is, in fact, stupendous. It is no accident that although our ancestors once marked time from creation, we now mark it from his birth, counting backward as well as forward from that event. He came, and the world was forever changed.

The hallmark of his coming was radical identification with those to whom he came. Though one with God, he became one with us. Though clothed with power, he laid it aside. Though unlimited, he embraced limitation—even to death.

We call it the miracle of Christmas. Yet that very phrase often serves as a polite cover-up. Indeed, we could just as well say the scandal of Christmas. For his radical identification with a broken world is a piercing call inviting us to the same. He calls us, too, to come and die. He invites us to become what others are so that they can become what we are, by his grace. "We always carry around in our body the death of Jesus, so that the life of Jesus may also be revealed in our body" (2 Corinthians 4:10).

While the greatest miracles in mission since Pentecost are all based squarely on his coming and his continued presence among us in the Holy Spirit, they are also based in the lives of men and women who go to others with that same radical identification. Though possessing all things, they do not grasp any of them. Though having a place, they are willing to leave all for another "home" here, there, anywhere.

What a testimony it would be if in the third millennium hundreds of brothers and sisters from the wealthiest nation on earth would truly enter in to that miracle of miracles, here in our neighborhoods and around the world!

If we did, what would Jesus do? One beautiful worship text has us singing, "We will dance on the streets that are golden, the glorious bride and the great Son of Man!"[12] One can only imagine that if we did, he would be dancing before we arrived (see Zephaniah 3:17).

THE CHALLENGE OF INCLUSION

Standing in line, the teenagers shared their raw, contagious joy. A few hours earlier they had joined thousands of others who met Jesus in new ways at an event called Acquire the Fire. Now their local congregation was rejoicing in the overflow. Even the sermon was postponed as one after another laughed, cried, and sometimes haltingly, sometimes effusively, opened their hearts.

Then I spied a mother. Slipping from her seat in the sanctuary, she moved behind her two adopted children standing in the line. With tears flowing, she laid one hand on the shoulder of each. Longingly, she was reaching out. I grieved for her, and I was moved by her mother's heart. But I also sensed a wall between her and them. It seemed clear that she was not really wanted there.

In a flash I saw it. Many times I had heard parents of adopted children say, "I love them just like I love my own biological children. As I know my heart, there's no difference in the way I treat them." And I believed them. Still do.

But in that flash of insight I understood that one cannot treat adopted children "just the same" as the biological and anticipate that they will receive the same amount of love. The mountain of rejection they carry as a result of having been in some way unattended or set aside by their natural parents is just too great.

They need more, much more. Listening, loving, forgiving, lavishing care. Then maybe, by the grace of God, they may hear the same message that the biological children have already heard: "I love you." And when it is finally heard, they often grasp it more deeply than anyone ever did who did not know their rejection.

So it is in the church.

Those of us who have grown up in some congregation or circle of congregations too easily assume that we have a place there. It is ours, we think, because we were born into it by natural birth.

Those who were not, those who enter from the "outside," have a different path to walk. For, like adoptive parents, we who were "born inside" often say to each other, "We accept them in just the same way we accept those whose parents and grandparents were part of this congregation from time immemorial. There is no difference."

Yet they too need more, much more. For in the millions of ethnic churches around the world only by the grace of God do ethnic majorities give and ethnic minorities receive the gift of full inclusion. It can happen, but only with "no ordinary love." For Jesus must be absolutely central.

The fundamental reality is that *all* of us are in fact adopted children (see Ephesians 1:5). The new family totally supersedes the old. The more fully we are seized by this truth, the less we are bound by this-world ethnicities.

May God unbind us.

Radical Faith

What is the source of a truly radical faith?

We admire Abraham and Moses for their lives of faith, which impacted all of human history. We see Jesus, and we see a train of his followers throughout the centuries who took steps that we now describe as radical. We describe the Anabaptists as the "radical reformation." And we look for their spiritual children in our generation, sometimes debating whether this or that expression is one of "radical Christianity." We search for the path of faithfulness. What does that look like?

Are the cross-cultural missionaries radical because they leave the security of one people group and go to another for the sake of those who have not heard? Are the true radicals those like the Christian Peacemaker Teams, who place themselves in violence-ridden places for the sake of reconciliation? Or are they those who dare to think new thoughts about God and act on them? Are they those who pray all night? Or are they those who place all their possessions in a common pool and share equally? Or those who give away ninety percent of their wealth and live on ten?

Whom shall we emulate? With whom shall we identify?

There will always be those in every human community who are deemed to be radical—those who throw caution to the wind, the blazers of new trails, those with a great passion who lay down their lives for its achievement or for the sake of others. The

Christian community, like others, will always have its radicals in this sense. By such evaluation, the Anabaptists were indeed radical, as are many mentioned above.

Yet our longing is for something more. We seek not merely some particular step of faithfulness to the heavenly vision, but we desire such conformity with the One who called us that heaven itself—not merely earth—smiles.

With that confession the answer to our question begins to come clear. We do not seek a reputation or a particular form of Christian faith. We do not aspire merely to great passion or great novelty. Our aim is not to leave a legacy. We may or may not be considered radical.

But we aspire to walk with God. We aspire to hear his voice and follow him. As we do, heaven smiles. Earth, we know, is fickle—for we are fickle. But our God is not.

To know him, to walk with him, to hear and respond in this generation. It is the only passion worth having.

BEING PERIPHERAL

"The church, you see, is not peripheral to the world; the world is peripheral to the church" (Ephesians 1:23, The Message). We will never see the glory of God in our generation unless we get our peripherals straight.

I read the newspaper, and there I am drawn to the centrality of the politics, art, science, sports, and entertainment of my time. The latest military adventure, the recent World Series surprise, the newest theater blockbuster—these grab my attention like a magnet. These are on center stage; they scream from the headlines.

I drive down the road and into the city, and I am overwhelmed by the very presence of the wealth of western civilization. State-of-the-art, finely sculpted automobiles crowd the roads of the countryside. Sky-scraping temples of finance and business brush the heavens as I drive into center city. I am small, but that very smallness is a comforting extension of the achievements of the human community.

I go home, and there I find an oasis of comfort amid the negative intrusions of the world beyond. Warmth, hot water, delicious food, the companionship of family and friends—what a gift! "Every man's home his palace" seems much more than an old English hope.

Yet all these are peripheral. Real, yes, but nevertheless peripheral to what this age scarcely recognizes. And what is that but the majestic yet humble presence of God, our Creator and Redeemer, who invites us away from the delusory attractions and distractions of all that we have created into the intimacy and fellowship of what he has created for us in Jesus our Savior and Lord? Our creations versus his creation. That is the issue.

"The church is Christ's body, in which he speaks and acts, by which he fills everything with his presence" (Ephesians 1:23, The Message).

Through prayer and intimate fellowship with God, through lives of constant turning, hearing, and obeying, we move to the periphery of our age. But in that move we find ourselves nearing the center of another reality. "The Lord is there" (Ezekiel 48:35).

The church will always be peripheral to the world and the vision of this age. We should not be surprised when we are marginalized, ignored, or shunned. Jesus knew all about that.

But we are not dismayed. For that which is the periphery of one reality is the center of another, and that new center is an unspeakably glorious new creation, pulsating with the transforming grace of the One who calls us into everlasting life.

Indeed, the church is not peripheral to the world; the world is peripheral to the church. Not in pride do we proclaim and live it, but in inexpressible gratitude. For this reason we pray, we send, we give, we go.

Pray, Listen, and Obey

After serving for more than a decade in mission administration, most of that time as vice president, Lamar Myers with his wife, Pat, are off to Bulgaria on a mission assignment. The mission office staff will miss him greatly, but we are grateful that they continue to be part of our international mission family.

During his years in administration, Lamar was a rock of gentleness, faithfulness, and servant leadership. He could always be counted on to greet each new challenge and relationship with his gracious, hallmark smile and warm spirit, coupled with a dry wit that let us know the presence of an active, engaging mind.

He was so gracious and kind that one could be tempted to think he sometimes lived in denial. But those of us who knew him best knew otherwise. He was deeply in touch with all that happened around him, but he carried spiritual resources that kept him steady like a gyroscope.

Though he was known in leadership meetings as one who rarely jumped into the fray of intense discussion and debate, we awaited, then carefully weighed, his incisive comments, which often produced little paradigm shifts of sudden illumination that led to wise decisions. I turned to him frequently for counsel when we were out of the public eye.

Lamar and Pat have spent their lifetime in mission. Significant chapters have been in Haiti with World Team, in Atlanta in World

Team mission administration, and most recently with Eastern Mennonite Missions. It was their deeply held evangelical Anabaptist commitments that led them here, and it is characteristic of their single-minded life focus that they move next to a mission frontier in Bulgaria.

In his final words as an officer to the board, Lamar told the story of two young Chinese Christian women who struck off to another part of China soon after their conversion, in obedience to Jesus' command to go. They were gone for two years, with no news trickling back home.

When they returned, it was only with great difficulty that their pastor pried from them the story of their mission. They had not done much, they said. Yet thirty new fellowships had been begun, the smallest 225 and the largest nearly five thousand in size.

"What did you do to begin these fellowships?" they were asked by their incredulous listeners.

"We didn't do anything," they responded. "We just prayed, and waited until the Holy Spirit told us to do something. We did that, and then prayed some more. When the Lord told us something more, we did that. That's all."

We sat in silence as the Lord spoke to us through Lamar that September morning in the meetinghouse. When he sat down, the meeting continued, but there was an almost palpable sense of the presence of God among us.

Thank you, Lamar.

LOSING MY FAITH

To become a follower of Jesus is to lose my faith. At least, that's what it meant for my Muslim friend. Little did I understand the agony he experienced when we first invited him into our home and together sang our Christian songs, read the New Testament, and prayed. That was more than twenty years ago, and I thought he was already a Christian.

But he was entrapped in an elaborate web of pretense not at all to his liking, created to protect himself, his Muslim peers, and his Christian friends. So although I thought him a Christian believer, he was still on a long journey to Jesus, wrestling with profound questions of identity, faith, and transparency.

He was a convinced Muslim, and his greatest fear was that by friendship with Christians he would lose his faith. To him, that faith was a priceless treasure, combining all the richness and security of God, nation, family, and personal identity. Yet whenever he was with Christians he experienced a strange joy and freedom that drew him back to their side again and again.

"Who am I?" he asked with increasing passion and perplexity.

Indeed, he would finally "lose his faith." Like Saul on the road to Damascus, he met the risen Christ in a life-transforming invitation into the new creation. He lost his faith and found his Lord. Today he is a sensitive, radiant herald of the good news, forever changed in union with Christ.

It strikes me, though, that losing one's faith is not the peculiar journey of a Muslim toward union with Jesus as Savior and Lord. It is, in fact, the journey of everyone whose life is transformed by coming to Jesus.

When Jesus walks among us, he still proclaims, "The kingdom of God has come near you." His servants still announce, "Repent, and be baptized, and you will receive the forgiveness of sins and be filled with the Holy Spirit."

But the message might well be translated, "Lose your faith! Lose your faith in your inherited religious forms and practices. Lose your faith in your parents' religion. Lose your faith in your own created theological constructs. Lose your faith in your nation and clan. Come to me!"

It is that radical message that by his grace we proclaim and live. Not because we have a superior culture, religion, or morality. It is precisely that sense of superiority and all that goes with it that we are called to lose.

What then do we gain when we lose our faith? Only this—eternal life in union with Jesus as Savior and Lord. Only this—the loss of all else to which we cling, thus becoming perpetual aliens in this world. Only this—divine transformation.

Reverse Culture Shock

You can't go home again. Country singers, soldiers, and wandering souls of every generation have always known it. You can't go home again because home changes and you change. Troth pledged under the stars becomes a distant memory and new realities supplant forgotten vows.

Cross-cultural missionaries know the agony of culture shock. Yes, there is the lure of the unknown, the excitement of beginning to learn a new language, the joy of hearing God's call and obeying. But after the excitement comes the sheer shock of it. One is stripped of old roles and relationships, and the stabilities of habits, customs, and social frameworks inherited from childhood are replaced with the uncertainties of the mysterious, arbitrary, and ruthless new world. No one seems to care, and those who do are ill equipped to understand. Depression sets in, or the worker takes refuge on expatriate islands, forgoing or delaying a deep bonding with the new community.

Yet year after year the dedicated witness lives on into the adopted new world, and slowly but surely a heart identification with a new people is forged while the old home recedes further into the past. Yet home, the way home was, remains an anchor, a memory, an inerasable and comforting familiarity deeper than consciousness.

Then, someday, we come home. But despite our fondest,

deepest-held familiarities and dreams, we can't do it. Home has changed and we have changed. The country singer and the traveling minstrel were right.

Oh sure, we can come back to the same places and to many of the same people. But the agony of the first culture shock we experienced in identifying with a new people in that other place is now measured and transcended by a new and deeper agony, for now it's harder to come home than it ever was to leave.

Social scientists call it reverse cultural shock. We expected the first, but the second caught us completely off guard. The congregation we left has changed more than they ever imagined. Dozens of faces are new; leadership is different; values have shifted; associations are transformed. Our old places are no longer vacant; others have filled them. What was priceless in the new world we just left behind is now of passing interest only; one Sunday evening program and all is duly noted.

Home? No . . . no . . . but yes! Those same skills and commitments painstakingly learned in going away are now to be thrice honed in returning. We go and come and go again, stripped and wounded—yet transformed in the power of the Spirit for every old and new home. *We can come home again!*

THE PEACE WE PROCLAIM

Mennonites, Brethren, and Quakers have been known for generations in the West as the historic peace churches because we did not send our young men to serve in the military. Yet simultaneously we have also maintained that we do not represent some minor eddy on the edge of the main stream of the Christian movement.

We point to other western groups of radical biblicists such as the Assemblies of God, who officially carried a "peace position" just like ours from their beginnings in the Pentecostal movement until 1968. We observe the Kimbanguists, a large prophetic African church whose leader taught the way of nonresistant love. We remember that D. L. Moody, the nineteenth-century evangelist, was a nonresistant Christian by conviction. And we trace the radical expressions of biblical Christianity through the centuries in groups like the Waldensians, Bohemian Brethren, and Moravian Brethren, who also proclaimed and lived the way of suffering love.

We also point to the commitments of Roman Catholic priests and members of religious orders to refrain from military service, and we confess that "we are all priests." In short, we believe that the way of peace is for the whole body of Christ.

What is the taproot of this peace we proclaim? Is it a philosophy of pacifism, a moral commitment to nonviolent resistance? Is it a well-honed ethic derived from a systematic explication of regard for others? Is it a conviction about the sacredness of human life? Does it derive from some list of do's and don'ts that we construct from Scripture? Is it based on our concept of justice? Is it an argument against "just war"?

No. Each of these may have its place in someone's apologetic for the peace of Christ. Yet none would have taken Jesus to the cross or would sustain the innumerable brothers and sisters who have faced dungeon, fire, and sword through the centuries since.

The peace we proclaim is rooted in God's forgiving love. Jesus expressed it supremely in his sacrificial death on the cross, and he calls us to follow his steps. Not, of course, that any of us can replicate his saving death, but that he continues to reach out in transforming, suffering love through his disciples in every century. He empowers us by his Spirit to love and to forgive—even our enemies.

This is the peace we proclaim, a peace that all our brothers and sisters in every century can readily understand, though not all apply it in the same ways. It is a peace that is expressed in thousands of ordinary and extraordinary ways in the body of Christ, not only in how we respond to military service. In fact, if that were our only touchstone for the gospel of peace, we would have already ceased to understand and live it.

Together with Christ, transforming the world.

WHAT KIND OF UNITY?

As diversity increases, unity is strained. Families, churches, communities, and nations all experience it.

Yet there are powerful bonds that hold together very diverse groups. Nation, language, faith, or blood—any of these can be a strong glue, but when perchance all are shared, it's a super-glue.

North American Mennonite Christians, like many others, know about superglue. Commonalities of faith and culture have combined to create an extraordinary sense of identity. It is a unity that results from radical faith, frequently supported by common ancestry.

But the faith is not always supported by common ancestry. During the past fifty years, Anabaptist churches, based on that radical New Testament faith, have blossomed in many new places, both in North America and around the world. As a result of this mission movement, these Christians now claim strikingly diverse biological ancestries.

As long as radical faith stays at the center, questions of common ancestry, while interesting, remain on the sideline. But when the faith weakens, other commonalities quickly replace it. One of those is ancestral. Others are traditional or cultural.

We are living in such an era. When we say, "Our church is increasingly diverse," we are sometimes referring to the new cultural diversity. At other times we mean diversity in faith or theology. So we are forced to ask, "What kind of diversity?"

Which immediately begs another question, "What kind of unity do we seek?" Is it the unity of common ancestry, common traditions, common organizational commitments? Or is it the unity of a common radical faith?

Our missionary commitment is clear. That which flings us into the world is passion for Jesus—to know him and to make him known. It is a radical New Testament faith. It accepts and even promotes all kinds of cultural and ancestral diversity. It accepts organizational diversity. But it rejects any diversity that strays from one Lord, one faith, one baptism, one God and Father of all.

A lay pastor in one of our congregations put it in grammatical terms.

> It's a matter of nouns and adjectives. *Christian* must be the noun. *Mennonite* or *charismatic* or *Anabaptist* must be the adjective. We may wholeheartedly be "Mennonite Christians." But when *Mennonite* becomes the noun, we're in trouble. Then we have "charismatic Mennonites," "peace and justice Mennonites," or "traditional Mennonites." Menno, not Christ, subtly becomes the center.

What kind of unity will we choose?

PART 4

THE WORLD

TODAY'S MISSION FRONTIERS

Where in the world are today's mission frontiers?

There are lots of nominees. For some, the frontiers are wherever one happens to live. Bloom where you're planted, they say. Every community in the world has needs—spiritual, emotional, material. Reach out to others where you live. That's your world, and that's where you will be most effective. Go to your own community.

For others, the frontiers are urban. Get to the city, they say. That's where the people are. That's where the greatest needs are. The early church apostles went to the cities, and from there the good news spread throughout the countryside. Don't waste your time in little places; go to the cities.

For still others, the frontiers are among the poor. Go to the poverty-stricken, the marginalized, the oppressed, they say. God has a heart for the poor; Jesus came to proclaim freedom for the oppressed. You don't first preach to a hungry world; rather, you give bread. That's where the real frontiers are; go to the poor. Others say the real frontiers point to youth, to leaders, to non-Christian world religions, to postmodern western society, or to indigenous peoples.

There is truth in all the claims and statistics aplenty to support every nominee. So where are the frontiers of today?

The answer is unchanged since the apostolic age. We go to those people(s) who have not yet heard and seen, to those places where there is not yet a viable, witnessing church. We look for those places of spiritual darkness and bondage, where people have least opportunity to hear and understand the good news. We go in obedience to the Holy Spirit.

The places may be near at hand; they may be far away. They may be urban; they may be rural. They may be poor; they may be wealthy. Through the centuries, the arenas change, but the commission remains the same: Go, make disciples of all peoples, baptizing, teaching.

At the beginning of the twenty-first century, our special focus remains on the 10/40 Window[13] pictured below. The global evangelical church has come to the realization that today most people who have never met a Christian, have never seen and have never heard the good news of Jesus Christ, live in this "window." Though there are also important frontiers in many other places, the evangelization of people in the 10/40 Window still presents us with our biggest challenge.

Other frontiers, of course, keep emerging, less defined by this geographic designation. One of the most ironic and troubling of these is the civilizational sea in which we ourselves swim—the West. Symbolic of this is Europe, still heading the list of continents in numbers of Christians, yet spiritually one of the neediest in the world.

So we go.

EVANGELISM, COME HOME

One of our goals for the new millennium is to send a cross-cultural missionary from every congregation. The vision is for each congregation to be caught up personally in both the joy and the mandate of global missions, not only praying and supporting those who go from our wider circles of fellowship but also commissioning and sending those whom the Lord calls and who now sit beside us Sunday after Sunday. Sons and daughters, nieces and nephews, brothers and sisters, bosom friends.

We know that if we do not send from among our most intimate circles of fellowship, we lose the immediacy, the urgency of Jesus' commission to disciple the nations. We begin to think of missions as something for the "professionals," for the mission board, for the relief agency, for somebody else out there. Eventually we can even question whether anyone need go.

Missions must come home. However, it's not going to happen unless evangelism first comes home. Unfortunately, we have gradually grown accustomed to limiting evangelism to what Billy Graham or Steve Wingfield does. It is an intercongregational ministry for the gifted person rather than a central function of each local body. Or it is someone else's personal spiritual gift. So how might evangelism come home?

There are, no doubt, many answers. But we could begin by identifying and commissioning at least one evangelist in every congregation to give leadership to the work of evangelism right at home.

Why not? For generations we have ordained pastors to give leadership to the work of shepherding the flock. Why not begin to ordain or commission evangelists to lead us in reaching out with the love of Christ to those around us, discipling new believers? Such persons would not replace pastors; they would complement them.

We do have a model. Ethiopian congregations commission evangelists as full-time workers even before they appoint pastors. Every established congregation has at least one, and many have several. Furthermore, these same evangelists not only lead the congregations in local evangelism but also oversee new church plantings in surrounding communities. Perhaps it goes without saying that these churches are growing like topsy.

In Ephesians 4:11 we read, "He gave some to be . . . evangelists." Though there is no lack of affirmation among us for the ministry of evangelism in the local congregation, a practical step remains—to commission evangelists.

It's not that they do not exist. They are there. Let's release and appoint them as the Spirit leads. If we do, it could revolutionize our life together.

When evangelism comes home, so will commitment to global missions.

A Defining Moment in Missions

In late August 1997 René Peñalba, then pastor of the Amor Viviente congregation of Tegucigalpa, Honduras, stood before the first of three Anabaptist mission study groups to Latin America, Africa, and Asia. As he outlined the mission vision of Amor Viviente, his words were crisp, moving. "We don't have the money," he said, "but we're going to go."

It was crystal clear that René was not asking North American mission organizations to underwrite Latin American missions. Rather, he was expressing the heart passion and commitment of brothers and sisters in Honduras to obey the final words of Jesus. The world will hear!

Since that moment, the message has become increasingly clear and unmistakable. Though René was not the first to articulate it, he brought the message home to us. The mission movement is now global. The Lausanne and AD 2000 movements, the great global consultations on world evangelization of the 1990s, the meteoric rise in numbers of cross-cultural missionaries from Africa, Asia, and Latin America, the chaotic but Spirit-led growth of mission by migration, the rapid growth of "insider movements"—all this and much, much more has thrust us into the new millennium even as we try to catch our breath from the speed of change.

For about five hundred years, Europeans and those of

European descent have played a central role in taking the good news to those who had not yet heard. But now, at the beginning of this millennium, we find ourselves surrounded by brothers and sisters from many nations who have a vision and passion for missions that matches anything we have ever experienced, even in the heady days after 1810, when U.S. churches sent their first foreign missionaries.

Indeed, we have become learners and followers, and rightly so. Not that we have no more to share or that we should cease sending workers in obedience to Christ. A thousand times, no. Rather, we are beginning to understand the mighty power that has been unleashed for world evangelization in faith communities on other continents where the mission is untainted by our blind spots.

Hailu Cherinet of Ethiopia, speaking at a Youth Evangelism Service commissioning in the late 1990s, captured it well:

> In the district of which I was overseer, we sent out evangelists who shared the gospel with two young men. The teenagers (ages fifteen and seventeen) were saved prior to this encounter. But they were inspired and revived during this meeting and started to pray the Scripture found in 1 John 4:4 [KJV]: "Greater is he that is in you, than he that is in the world." They immediately went to the spiritual power center of that region, where a witch doctor ruled with demonic power, and began to take authority in the name of Jesus. For three weeks, they walked around it, praying.
>
> At the end of three weeks, the witch doctor systematically began to tear down the building in which he worked, saying that his power to work in that place was gone. As a result, 200 families (822 persons) were saved.

Hailu sent three different emissaries to verify the story before he believed it.

THE PRESENCE OF JESUS IN A POST-CHRISTIAN WORLD

These days, Christian intellectuals are intrigued with the fact that the western world is "post-Christian." In its simplest form, this argument says that Christianity has been tried and found wanting by our culture, hence conversion to Christ is much more difficult here than in other places, where the good news is still new. Or in other words, we have, in the opinion of many, moved beyond Christ.

As a result, some of our finest missiologists are focusing our attention on the importance of Christian witness in the western world. One is Wilbert Shenk, professor emeritus of the School of Intercultural Studies at Fuller Theological Seminary. Another is David Shenk, missionary and global resource to the burgeoning churches and mission movements of Africa, Asia, and Latin America. Both men have spent much of their lives focusing missionary attention on other parts of the world, but they carry an increasingly deep conviction that witness in the context of European-American culture is one of our most important, and challenging, modern mission frontiers.

It is a welcome to the real world.

We've known for centuries that Europe and the United States are not really Christian, that Christendom—that is, state-church Christianity—is not synonymous with the kingdom of heaven.

Yet we have treasured, too much perhaps, the special privileges that come to evangelical Christians in societies that have been profoundly shaped by the presence of the church—and have even come to take these privileges for granted.

But most of our brothers and sisters, in most centuries and in most places since Pentecost, have experienced the church as an essentially missionary community in an often hostile environment. Why should we assume it to be any different where we live?

If our world is indeed progressively understood as post-Christian, perhaps we should just bow in humble gratitude to God, putting away forever our rose-tinted glasses. After all, the New Testament is quite clear that there are just two real kingdoms: the kingdom of light and the kingdom of darkness. To identify fully any earthly political entity with either of these is already to be misled.

So welcome to the post-Christian world. The real world.

We take our place with suffering, enduring brothers and sisters in every age and in every part of our world today, knowing that the church of Christ is essentially a missionary community. The world does not and cannot understand it—whether we live in the United States, France, the Sudan, Northern Ireland, Kenya, or Indonesia. We do not expect to dominate but to win with suffering love.

If we are sometimes tempted with a sense of loneliness in facing issues of post-Christianity or postmodernity unique among the Christian communities of our world, let's not forget that many others before us have walked the same path. Most of the ancient Christian communities around the Mediterranean, for example, eventually had to learn what it meant to live in a post-Christian world, dwelling for centuries in regions that had once been dominantly Christian but were no longer. Where, for example, are the "seven churches of Revelation" today?

Indeed, the necessity to take our places with vision and hope in a thoroughly post-Christian world could help reintroduce us to what God all along intended for us to be. That would be a gift.

Missions: The New Era

As we have seen, until about 1990, European and North American churches could justifiably consider themselves to be the primary cross-cultural Christian missionary sending centers of the world. Here missionaries were prayed forth, trained, and sent. From here they were supported, and to here most of them returned to report and eventually to retire, if they lived long enough.

Here were the Bible institutes and colleges, the missiologists, and the support frameworks for the "missionary enterprise." Here were the addresses of most mission sending organizations, and here were the sending churches. Many are still here.

Yet something has fundamentally changed. Today, European and North American missionary sending organizations have been joined by thousands of new sending centers in Latin America, Africa, and Asia. And now when the global numbers of cross-cultural missionaries are reported, tens of thousands come from those continents.

Today Christian mission is global, not only because it is to the world but also because it is from the world.

Of course, we've used this language about the Christian church for many decades. In the twentieth century William Temple, archbishop of Canterbury from 1942 to 1944, spoke of the "great new fact of our time," that the Christian church has become a truly universal religion. The ecumenical movement of the first half of the twentieth century set out to express the oneness of this emerging global community of faith. Yet even as that movement attempted to embody the unity of Christ, it faltered in expressing the missionary heart of God. As a result, it began to lose its reason for being.

Thus while we could then speak of a global church, to talk of the global church in mission was premature. No longer.

Almost suddenly, we see the churches of Latin America, Africa, and Asia beginning to take the lead in cross-cultural missionary sending. In our circles, the emergence in 1997 in Calcutta of the International Missions Association including Hondurans, Ethiopians, and Indonesians is one expression. But that's only the tip of the iceberg.

Everywhere we go in missions, we meet them. Koreans, Indians, Latin Americans, Africans. Not serving with western mission organizations anymore but sent from their own centers of mission. Not trained in North America but mentored in their own schools by their own leaders.

For decades we in the West tended to think of them as having a special mission to their own culture groups. Of course, they did, just as we did to ours. But Jesus has spoken the great commission to them just as clearly as he ever did to us, and now they are going as cross-cultural messengers to still other cultures.

It's a new era in missions. Brothers and sisters are taking the good news from the whole world to the whole world. It's a day of rejoicing—a time to press on and not to falter.

How the Gospel Came to My People

My ancestry is Swiss-German. Each time I return to western Europe, I realize that I'm walking among my distant cousins. At the turn of the century, when I was participating in a youth convention in Detmold, Germany, I met a young Mennonite evangelist named Armin Schowalter, whose father had sent a note confirming that we were indeed part of the same family. Our common ancestors lived in Strengelbach, Switzerland, at the time of the Anabaptist movement.

Armin's sister smiled when we were introduced. "I can tell you're a Schowalter," she said. "After nine generations you still have a crooked nose!" She then explained that the Schowalters of the Palatinate are known for noses that tilt to the left. Suddenly, and for the first time in my life, I felt a wave of gratitude for my crooked nose.

Many North American Anabaptists trace our spiritual roots back to Switzerland, Germany, and Holland—back to those sixteenth-century radicals who lived and died with such passionate, wholehearted commitment to Jesus and to the world for which he died. They left a thrilling legacy to the church around the world.

Yet each time we read the Bible, we are reminded that these spiritual roots go far beyond that, right back to Peter and Paul, back to Jesus, back to Abraham and Sarah. So how did the Europeans first hear the good news?

As we can partially reconstruct the story these many centuries later, it was Celtic evangelists from the British Isles who first carried the good news to many Germanic tribes, eight hundred years before Martin Luther, Michael Sattler, and Hans de Ries. The Celts were a group of tribes extending all the way from ancient Galatia, where Paul preached, through parts of continental Europe to modern Wales, Ireland, and Scotland.

These Celtic Christians were fervent followers of Jesus, just as their spiritual descendants during the European Reformation would be centuries later. They were a people of prayer, holiness, passion for the Word, and a deep desire to share the good news with those who had not yet heard. Like their spiritual descendants, they were willing to live and die for the sake of Jesus. They called their missionaries "wanderers."

So, those of Swiss-German ancestry, it was Celtic foreign missionaries who first came to our ancestors. Thank God for the Welsh, Irish, and Scottish. Their ancestors, the Celts, introduced ours to Jesus.[14]

In turn, whatever our ancestry, we owe a tremendous debt of gratitude to all the believers churches of continental Europe, and especially to those faithful congregations that have persisted through the centuries. They have pressed on in faithfulness to Jesus—crooked noses and all—in spite of many handicaps and long periods of opposition.

In the past century it has been our joy to rejoin them in mission to Europe and to the world. We are connected! From people to people the story continues, until Jesus returns. Thank you, Europe. Thank you, God.

AT HOME ONCE AGAIN

It is no accident that Eastern Mennonite Missions began as Home Missions Advocates in 1894. Mission always begins at home.

It is true that for the past couple hundred years we've associated missions with "foreign missions," and some people are led to Christ by foreigners. Sometimes that's us when we go; sometimes it's us when they come our way. Meeting Jesus through the witness of foreigners, however, is relatively rare.

Most people meet Jesus within their own cultural wombs, and most movements of mission begin there too—at home. Furthermore, unless each new generation is being evangelized, mission movements from that particular place will quickly cease.

At the beginning of this century, we're coming back home. Not that we cease going to other parts of the world. By the grace of God, we will continue and strengthen that obedient faith.

But we sense the need for new movements of outreach right where we live. We are challenged to become missional. Patrick Keifert, Lutheran "bishop" to Lancaster Mennonite Conference and leader of a consulting group called Church Innovations, says that a congregation becomes truly missional when it as much "church sent" as it is "church gathered."[15] Here and there we are breaking out of crusty cocoons.

We are inspired by new centers of evangelism and mission emerging in cities like Philadelphia, Birmingham, and New York.

With joy, we continue to help send church-planting teams to many locations. Our gatherings are changing; more of our last names are mutually unpronounceable; our vision is enlarged.

Yet we are a people in need of revival. The stirring of the Holy Spirit among us is real and deep. Transformed lives? There are many.

But the challenge we face in our own nation is enormous. Churches are born, and churches die. But more die than are born. The society around us seems less hospitable to the good news now than we think it was a century ago. The Bible is less well known. Many new churches are born simply because so many old ones are dying, not primarily because of evangelism. We face a post-Christian postmodern society.

Far from giving less attention to spiritual needs in the United States, we are committed to giving more. We must become a missional church here, where we live.

We will continue to focus on outreach in the United States, for unless we are dynamic, outreaching congregations at home, any hope of sharing the good news in other parts of the world is dead. We believe that bringing down the artificial walls between "home" and "overseas" will increase the vitality and focus of what we do at home as well as overseas.

Thirty Miles from the Nearest Missionary

"What's in the DNA of Eastern Mennonite Missions?"

I've heard the question, and helped to answer it, many times. In the past decade, the answers we give usually have something to do with multiplication—of disciples, churches, ministries, mission-sending groups.

One could argue, as we do, that if we were not about multiplication, we would not be a mission-sending society. Multiplication is at the heart of missions.

But the DNA of an organization is complex and many-faceted. Another aspect of missions DNA is location. Where do we send workers? To the communities where we already have churches in the United States? To places in our country we have not yet gone? To other parts of the world?

We've stressed that our primary destination is to our home communities, then to other parts of the United States, then to other nations. Missions to the "regions beyond" are the overflow of the zeal and calling that the Holy Spirit gives us for our own backyards. It's a way of reading Acts 1:8.

Furthermore, that's the way it actually happened. EMM started in 1894 as Home Missions Advocates. It started Sunday schools and new fellowships, first in Lancaster County, Pennsylvania, then Philadelphia, then other parts of the country. Only much later, in 1934, did we send our first witnesses abroad—to Tanganyika, East Africa.

However, a prominent organizer of the Home Missions Advocates was J. A. Ressler, who was twenty-seven when the organization was founded in 1894. Five years later, he was in India leading the first three missionaries sent abroad by the Mennonite Board of Missions of Elkhart, Indiana. His instructions? "Go to India and locate at least thirty miles from the nearest missionary." For the next forty years, Lancaster Conference Mennonites, especially in the Paradise District, were vigorous supporters of the India mission.

What's my point? Simply this—that mission to unreached peoples was part of our DNA from its very beginning. Home missions is in our DNA too, and mission means multiplication. But even more specifically, the vision that fired the twelve young men and their families who seeded this mission society in 1894 was already a vision for those who had not yet heard, to the ends of the earth. We had already read all of Acts 1:8, the end as well as the beginning.

"Thirty miles from the nearest missionary." At the beginning of a new millennium, those places still exist geographically, culturally, and spiritually. Those are still the frontiers, at home and abroad.

In obedience to Jesus, we still go.

Why Should We Take Good News to 'Resistant Peoples'?

Often the question is asked, Why should we send witnesses to the Muslim world? Everyone knows Muslims are not responding to Jesus like Latin Americans are, or like non-Muslim sub-Saharan Africans. Shouldn't we go to places where the harvest is ripe, where there'll be more fruit? It doesn't make sense to sow the seed in places where the ground is hard and stony. Let's find the good soil and go there. Doesn't the Holy Spirit lead us to prepared people? It's a sign of not hearing God to spend years working somewhere without fruit. Didn't Jesus say to shake the dust off your feet and move on if you're not received?

These are compelling questions, at least on the surface. Effectiveness, timing, and spiritual sensitivity seem to make it clear that we shouldn't spend much time with "resistant peoples."

Yet there is another side, a side where God must often weep, a side we must ponder long and hard. Many of the "resistant" are simply neglected. We assume they're resistant because they did not respond seven hundred or even fifty years ago. We assume they're resistant because they do not respond quickly.

Yet many of these have never met a vibrant, witnessing Christian. Many have never understood who Jesus is. Dare we assume they are resistant because of choices their ancestors made?

We also assume they're resistant because sometimes their governments attempt to shield them from Christian witness. They're hard to get to. Yet we know that a government posture does not automatically define the posture of the people who live under it. Remember the Reformation radicals. Remember the Ethiopians of the 1930s and 1980s. Remember the Chinese of the 1970s.

The resistant, in fact, are often not what they appear to be. We assume that appearances don't deceive. We assume that the Spirit normally takes us only to people who initially receive us warmly. And we assume once resistant, always resistant.

But we know better. We know that the policies of a national government do not determine the spiritual receptivity of its citizens. We know that the roughest exterior often conceals the softest heart. We know that people, even resistant people, can change. Often, in fact, they change more quickly and more radically than those who appear to be more open. And we know that Jesus never promised us we wouldn't suffer.

And finally, the truly receptive may be camouflaged by the truly resistant. We assume that all the people in a given cultural group are more or less alike. We assume that we can typecast a whole family network by the dominant leaders within it.

But we know that this is not true. We know that every people group, but not all of every group, will be around the throne of God. We know that Jesus came to bring division as well as unity. We know that members of the same human family will take different paths.

So we refuse to be captured by the dominant success motif of our culture. By the grace of God, we will not choose to go simply on the basis of the most fruit, the largest harvest, the most rapid results. Rather, we also go to the neglected, the hostile, the difficult. We go to the poorest of the poor. We go to the resistant. We go to the fringes.

And Jesus goes before us.

APOSTOLIC BANDS

How has the world Christian movement taken root in so many different cultures? Has it been a spontaneous expansion of churches, powered by the Holy Spirit? Has it been the quiet, persistent witness of ordinary believers who go from place to place as merchants, maids, prisoners, slaves, or scholars? Has it resulted from intrepid wanderers and apostles who go with passionate vision to reach the unreached, spurning the comforts of their native homes? Has it sprung somehow from the military conquests of Christian nations?

The world Christian movement is as complex and creative as the heart of God. It springs, after all, from God's mission, not ours. It is not limited to any of the forms we use to define or pattern it. It cannot be captured in any of our theoretical constructs.

Yet in spite of this unpredictability, we can say that one of the most persistent patterns of cross-cultural Christian expansion is that of the apostolic band. In the New Testament, we see Jesus first sending the twelve out two by two (see Mark 6:7-13), then seventy others, also two by two (see Luke 10:1-17). Later, the mission to the Gentiles follows the same pattern with Paul and Barnabas (see Acts 13:2).

In the centuries since, such teams of Christians, or missionary bands, have repeatedly catalyzed new circles of churches in new cultures. The monastic movements of the Church of the

East, Orthodox, and Roman Catholic churches were missionary at their core. More than a thousand years ago, John of Resh-aina and Thomas the Tanner took the good news from Persia to the Turks of Central Asia, Cyril and Methodius took the gospel from Greece to the Bulgarians, Frumentius and Aedesius from Syria to Ethiopia, Winfrith and his companions from Celtic communities in England to Germany.[16]

In the past five hundred years, the stream of such teams has grown rapidly, until today no one can fully measure it.

We follow in that train. Decades ago, we sent missionary bands to places like Tanzania, Ethiopia, Somalia, Kenya, Honduras, and Guatemala. Today new bands continue to go, with destinations like Thailand, Cambodia, and Central Asia.

The goal? To see the formation of circles of Christian churches in places where the church is weak or nonexistent. We call this "mission-to-world" to distinguish it from the vast amount of "mission work" focused on previously existing circles of churches, these often in places where the Christian witness is already quite strong. Around these mission-to-world missionary bands, new circles of churches are constantly springing up, some quickly, some more slowly.

How long does it take to see vibrant new circles of churches in a place where before there were none? Sometimes a decade, sometimes five, sometimes ten. On rare occasions, new circles of churches even seem to spring into existence almost full-blown. The pace varies widely, depending on the culture. But usually more than one missionary generation passes before rapid church multiplication begins. When it does begin, we call it a "church-planting movement" or a "movement to Jesus."

Two recent examples occurred among the Quechua of Peru and the Isaan of Thailand. In both places, new regional circles of churches emerged since the beginning of the twenty-first century. Both are crossing the threshold of becoming movements.

Of course, we enthusiastically send fraternal workers to walk alongside these existing circles of churches, especially when they have grown up around the witness of missionary bands we have sent. For then a strong spiritual bond already exists between us, an apostolic bond. This bond is the spiritual link between "parents" and "children" in Christ, between the messenger of the gospel and the recipient. We call these our mission-with-church relationships.

In Tanzania, Ethiopia, Kenya, Honduras, Guatemala, and the Philippines we have such mission-with-church relationships. We and the churches we represent in North America have powerful links with these circles of churches, links that both they and we together treasure. Together we pray, we assist, we learn. According to request, we send long-term fraternal workers; from the Lancaster Mennonite Conference, we send bishop fraternal representatives.

There is a further stage. These circles of churches form support structures to send their own missionary bands to still other places of spiritual need. New mission structures are formed as they send cross-cultural witnesses. We naturally link with these emerging mission groups, calling these our "mission-with-mission" relationships. Together with them we are exploring and implementing cross-cultural partnership in many places, going to places where the church is weak or nonexistent.

How then will global mission appear in the middle of the twenty-first century? No one yet knows. But one thing is sure. It is a new day, with a whole new set of relationships in mission. At the beginning of the twentieth century we were a tiny group of five thousand people in our congregations—alone, but beginning to reach out. At the beginning of the twenty-first century we are nearly twenty thousand, but we are now linked in mission with a quarter of a million others on four continents.

Serving God, together we go.

How Islam Led Me to Jesus

In Cairo at the northeastern tip of North Africa a Sudanese believer described how he met Jesus.

"Islam," he said, "was an important part of my journey to faith. The story of how God provided a lamb for Abraham was familiar to me from my Muslim childhood. Then later when I heard that Jesus was the Lamb of God, I understood immediately, and I believed.

"The hardest thing for me as a new believer was when I felt Christians wanted me to say negative things about Islam. For I am a Muslim follower of Jesus. To be sure, my family thinks I am a 'confused Muslim,' but nevertheless they receive me and hear my testimony. I think that if a Muslim comes to believe in Jesus as the Messiah, that's the bottom line."

A few days later, on the other side of North Africa, a follower of Jesus in Morocco shared a similar testimony.

"As a young man I received a deep conviction of my sinfulness," he said. "From my Muslim upbringing I knew that Jesus would return to earth someday, and I realized that I was not ready to meet him. As a result, I asked my boss for time off from work to seek peace."

Some time later, as a Christian friend read from Romans 8:1 that "there is no condemnation," he understood God's provision, and his conviction of sin was replaced by peace.

Both these brothers have a profound "at-homeness" in their Muslim communities, even while experiencing the peace that comes from knowing Jesus as Savior. Like other brothers and sisters in the Muslim world, they are in some sense Muslim Christians or Muslim believers in Jesus.

This is a step beyond what most western Christians are accustomed to thinking. We tend rather to draw sharp contrasts between Islam and Christianity. For example, we refer to "Muslim-background believers," not to Muslim believers in Jesus.

Yet I am moved as I encounter radical followers of Jesus in the Muslim world, men and women who have suffered for the sake of Christ, but who simultaneously refuse to reject their Muslim identity.

Is God preparing to unleash a new fire within the Muslim world as he has within the Jewish world? Will a new generation of believers decisively identify themselves as Muslim followers of Jesus rather than as Christians in some eastern or western sense?

I wonder.

BACK TO JERUSALEM

The goal—to send 100,000 Christian witnesses westward from China. The senders—the eighty million Christians of China. The vision—to complete the evangelization of the world.

During the past century many groups, and even individuals, have launched faith-filled plans for world evangelization. Perhaps the best-known recent such plan was that of the AD 2000 and Beyond movement. This movement convened a great gathering in Seoul in 1995 called the Global Consultation on World Evangelization—a taste of heaven on earth with 185 nations represented. And there have been many others.

But few have had such electrifying impact as the news from China. In books such as *Jesus in Beijing* by David Aikman and *Back to Jerusalem* by Paul Hattaway, the story is emerging.[17] From a suffering church comes a courageous vision, to take the good news into the center of what we westerners have dubbed the 10/40 Window, that part of the world in which most of the world's unreached peoples are found.

How was it determined to send 100,000? Their answer is clear. It is a tithe of the one million local leaders of the house churches of China. Why back to Jerusalem? Because, they say, the good news has been carried westward from Jerusalem through the centuries until it reached China. Now it is China's turn to continue the pilgrimage, completing the missionary circuit of the globe.

To the cynical westerner the vision of our Chinese brothers and sisters may seem like one more triumphalistic pipe dream of overenthusiastic Christians. Back to Jerusalem indeed! Into and through the heart of the Muslim, Buddhist, and Hindu worlds? One hundred thousand witnesses?

There may be a thousand reasons why it won't work. But our Chinese brothers and sisters remind us that the growth of the church in China was also "impossible," that they have counted the cost, and that unlike us they already know the meaning of suffering.

"In our mission training schools," they say, "we teach candidates how to get out of handcuffs in thirty seconds and how to jump from the second floor without breaking a leg."

Our dear Chinese brothers and sisters, we are praying for you. And we are praying with you. Press on—back to Jerusalem.

PART 5

THE PATH AHEAD

REVIVAL AND MISSIONS

"Revival is simply a new beginning of obedience to God."

With these matter-of-fact words and others like them, evangelist Charles Finney set forth his lawyer-like case for "revivals of religion" in early nineteenth-century America. He himself had met Christ as a twenty-something lawyer practicing in a small, upstate New York village near the present Mennonite communities around Lowville and Croghan. And neither his life nor the life of his nation would be quite the same.

He quickly challenged the reigning notion of his contemporaries, inherited from Jonathan Edwards, that revivals erupted mysteriously and unpredictably from sovereign visitations of the Holy Spirit entirely apart form human initiatives.

"You sow revivals like you sow seed in a field," Finney said. Revival time is any time. Any time men and women return to God, repenting and confessing their sins, they will receive divine visitations. Few could argue with Finney, for everywhere he traveled and preached, entire communities were moved to repentance and lives were changed, often dramatically.

Even as Finney preached, the modern evangelical mission movement was also getting underway. Pioneers like William Carey in India and Adoniram Judson in Burma were being used by God to awake the consciences of their fellow believers in Europe and the United States to their responsibility for preaching to those who had never heard. In the next 150 years, the good news circled the globe like never before since Pentecost. Revivals fed the missions movement.

In the generation after Finney, another American preacher, D. L. Moody, preached the love of God much as Finney had preached repentance. By Moody's time, German-American descendants of the Anabaptists were ready to enter more fully into the renewal streams that were influencing their English-speaking brothers and sisters.

Evangelists like J. S. Coffman and A. D. Wenger came into Mennonite communities, preaching repentance and the new birth, using the same patterns as Finney and Moody. In their days, we underwent a profound spiritual revolution, beginning in the 1880s. And what eventually became Eastern Mennonite Missions was born.

On into the twentieth century, the evangelical mission movement continued, accompanied by the revivals at home that we gradually came to believe we could simply "have." Slowly, imperceptibly, revival was more connected to its forms than to its substance. Revivals were scheduled, but often without repentance.

Yet the creativity and the in-breaking power of God surges across the embankments of human formalism in every generation. When revival becomes a mere form, the Holy Spirit simply finds a new path for renewal. Likewise when mission flows from fossilized, traditional remains of previous vital movements of the Spirit, God moves in power to create new vehicles for his love. Throughout the twentieth century, this has happened over and over again.

For example, when the nineteenth-century revival movements sparked by Finney, Moody, and others began to wane in the early twentieth century, the Pentecostal movement burst onto the scene with such energy that its effects were felt around the world, creating and releasing a flood of new mission vision and activity. Again at mid-century, when much of the Pentecostal movement was afflicted with hardening of the arteries, the charismatic renewal swept through mainline denominations, bringing a fresh vision of the heart of God. That prepared the way for the Jesus movement of the 1970s, which in turn galvanized a significant minority of the '60s generation. Many frontier missionaries of the 1970s and '80s found their spiritual home and calling to the harvest through the Jesus movement.

But these widely influential western movements were only a tiny part of the multifaceted work of God in renewal and mission. In Latin America, Africa, and Asia, many young churches planted by European and North American missionaries blossomed and grew beyond anticipation.

New revival movements in Africa, like the East African Revival, the Kimbanguists (Central Africa), and Kwasizabantu (South Africa), rebounded to bless the western world. In China, the Little Flock connected with Watchman Nee and others was internationally influential. Likewise, the teaching and preaching of twentieth-century Indian saints Sadhu Sundar Singh and Bakht Singh shook their nation and sent spiritual waves around the world. From South Korea, David Yonggi Cho became a legend in Christian households everywhere with his congregation numbering hundreds of thousands.

And what about our western congregations? Were the nineteenth-century revivals the last to touch them? Have mission groups like ours continued for a century only on the spiritual capital of that era?

Certainly not. The Catholic, Protestant, and Anabaptist Reformation movements have continued to exert their powerful influence upon us. The nineteenth-century renewals merged with Anabaptism in the Mennonite churches to reinvigorate that older but still strong stream. Other renewal streams have continued to flow in over the past decades.

For example, the East African Revival Movement influenced our work in foreign missions in the 1940s and the 1950s. Then in the 1970s and 1980s we were touched by the charismatic renewal.

Now at the beginning in the new millennium, such movements of the Spirit as that in the Christ's Foundation Church of Ethiopia sweep back to challenge and strengthen our faith.

For the future, where do we look for the new? Is it in waiting for the sovereign in-breaking power of God (Edwards) or in initiating a new beginning of obedience (Finney)? Is it transparency before the cross of Christ (East African Revival) or in receiving the power of the Spirit (Pentecostalism; charismatic renewal)? Is it a renewal of still more ancient visions, whether within the post-apostolic church or the medieval and Reformation radical communities of faith?

It is in all these and more! It is everywhere the living God touches and changes the human heart through the presence of the risen Christ. God is the great initiator, but he will not complete his work without a response of repentant faith. He reaches out in a thousand ways, and we may understand and receive in a thousand ways, but the result is one. New life in Christ. A whole new creation.

So we look for the new everywhere. Among our youth, our aged, within our congregations and beyond them. In North America, and in every other part of the world. Wherever God is transforming lives and creating new communities, there we learn, and there we rejoice.

THE INTERNATIONAL MISSIONS ASSOCIATION: MISSION FROM EVERYWHERE TO EVERYWHERE

We have seen repeatedly that an old chapter has ended, a new chapter has begun. For the last thousand years, the vision for Christian missions has been carried largely by Europeans. With the exception of the early missionary movement east of the Roman Empire through the Church of the East, whether Eastern Orthodox, Roman Catholic, Protestant, or evangelical, cross-cultural missionaries largely bore European names.

No longer. At the end of the twentieth century, Christian missionaries began bearing names from every continent and from most nations of the world. The church has become a truly global phenomenon, and wherever the church exists and the Holy Spirit indwells his people, there Jesus' great commission is heard and obeyed.

Today there are as many cross-cultural missionaries from the two-thirds world as there are of European descent. Given these trends, there will be many more tomorrow.

In Calcutta in January 1997, mission representatives of Anabaptist churches in Indonesia, Ethiopia, and the United States gathered in a classroom on the grounds of the Mennonite World Conference to form the International Missions Association (IMA).

Together with one absentee participant from Honduras, we formed a fledgling association of mission groups representing in Asia, Africa, Latin America, and North America.

Our goal was simple: to foster prayer, fellowship, and partnership in cross-cultural missions, with destinations especially among those peoples and places where the church is weak or nonexistent. For many years we had been related through mission from the United States; now we were expressing a heart desire to walk together as peers in mission to other parts of the world.

Already there is maturing fruit. By 2008 there were eighteen members of the association, and in the meantime, six years after its birth, the Global Mission Fellowship, a larger body representing Anabaptist mission groups globally, was born in Zimbabwe at the Mennonite World Conference assembly in 2003. Also simultaneously with the IMA, a similar group focused on short-term discipleship training and mission, the Global Discipleship Training Alliance, met for the first time in Atlanta. It has begun to grow rapidly, spreading among the burgeoning churches of the global south.

These are small, but significant, expressions of an emerging global phenomenon—mission from everywhere to everywhere. No longer is the primary initiative coming from North America or Europe. Rather, the vision for making disciples of all peoples is increasingly owned by vibrant, Jesus-centered churches and mission groups in every part of the world.

Together, we go.

The Coming of Peace and Justice

In the nineteenth century, missionaries and other westerners some-times debated the question "Which comes first, evangelization or civilization?" By civilization, they usually meant western civiliza-tion. In some cases they believed that civilization should come first, though most of them were quite ready to begin by telling the gospel story.

In the twentieth century, that question was mostly set aside for another similar discussion. "Is true evangelization possible without a parallel concern for development?" By development, we usually meant the technical, medical, and economic fruits of western civilization. By true evangelization, we meant holism, the concern for the whole person.

In both centuries, passions flared as missionaries were often accused of transporting their cultural baggage to other lands, whether in the form of civilization or development. They were accused of being unconcerned for the whole person. It seemed as though missionaries were damned if they did and damned if they didn't. Sometimes missionaries lined up on opposite sides with apparently contradictory answers.

But what does all that have to do with peace and justice?

Just this, that in the last third of the twentieth century, a con-cern for peace and justice emerged as a similar, and sometimes equally polarizing, new agenda for missionaries. Western missionaries especially saw this concern as something that should be exported wherever possible. Because of their historic peace witness, Anabaptist Christians took up this torch almost as though it were particularly native to them. Yet peace and justice is, like civilization in the 1800s and development in the 1900s, a potential red herring.

Will it likewise occupy the attention of a whole century? Maybe. In any case, it is not unlike the others. Missionaries today are judged to be imperfect if they do not espouse a high commitment to peace and justice, just as they were judged imperfect in the 1900s if they did not espouse a holistic commitment to development, and in the 1800s if they did not join the colonizers in promoting western civilization.

All of these are indeed noble aims. Each can be espoused with integrity by a western missionary. But the hazard of each has been that it is also profoundly shaped by western culture, with many other-than-Christian elements.

Do we then cast aside the concerns for civilization, development, or peace and justice? Certainly not. Jesus is the prince of peace. The gospel is the good news of reconciliation. The righteousness of God leading to human wholeness is there on virtually every page of Scripture. Real transformation is possible through Jesus our Lord.

But we go in mission with the humility born of the knowledge that wherever we introduce the Prince of Peace, we too will learn to know him all over again, in new depth. For our best packages are not yet complete.

Native Missionaries

These days I often hear the question, Why shouldn't we just give all our mission money for native missionaries?

Why not, indeed? If it costs, say, forty thousand dollars to send one North American missionary, but a local evangelist somewhere in India could do the same job for say four thousand, why spend ten times as much to send the North American with all the extra support and transportation costs? Let's be good stewards and support the Indian. The North American can stay home.

The question begs a thoughtful, honest answer.

Let's acknowledge that sometimes we should indeed stay home. No one should go anywhere and everywhere just because they have the financial capability to do so. That is spiritual imperialism of the worst sort. In fact, we frequently make decisions to leave particular places of mission for exactly this reason; we believe it's time for local evangelists, pastors, and missionaries to do what they can do better than we can. Our programs are designed for us to leave rather than to stay indefinitely.

Similarly, we must continue to examine the costs we incur in sending and going—particularly as we live in a wealthy nation with a high standard of living. We talk and pray about this often. But we also know that if we ceased modeling what we teach by sending dollars but not people, our very message would lose its impact.

We have a long history and passion for sending witnesses called by God to places where the church is weak or nonexistent. From inception, we have taken seriously Jesus' call to "make disciples of all nations." Our goal is to share God's love by introducing Jesus in ways that multiply both local and cross-cultural witnesses, everywhere God leads us. This is at the very center of our sending—to help catalyze vital, multiplying circles of congregations at home in their own cultures.

So a primary way we spend funds given to missions is in fact to create "native missionaries." North American missionaries go with this purpose, to witness in word, deed, and being. We desire to plant new congregations of believers who will then reach out to their neighbors and beyond.

We give both to support those we send and to share with our brothers and sisters. Twice in the first decade of the twenty-first century, for example, we sent tithes from large estate gifts for use by native missionaries in twenty mission groups around the world. We pioneer and partner with both people and funds.

Finally, let's not forget that North Americans are also native missionaries. Natives of here and natives in India are both called to local and cross-cultural mission. It is only as God mingles people, prayer, finances, vision, and gifts from every nation, including North America, in one great global symphony that Jesus will return in glory.

THE SECRET OF LIFT

At the beginning of the industrial revolution, when we still walked or were carried by horsepower, the first self-propelled road vehicle powered by steam was developed in France in 1769, followed in 1804 by the invention of steam locomotives for use on tramways in Wales. Next was an electric car in the 1830s, followed by the invention of the modern automobile by a German named Daimler in 1885.

But if the nineteenth century was full of new movement on the ground, a greater transformation was yet to come. In 1903 the Americans Samuel Langley and the Wright brothers took the magnificent, history-changing leap into the air with their inventions. They ushered in the age of flight with the heavier-than-air, gasoline-powered devices called airplanes. In a little more than a century, humanity had moved from mechanical locomotion on the ground to powerful, rapid locomotion through the air.

How? We had employed the secret of lift. In simple terms, an airplane stays up because its wings push the air down. Only by understanding and applying this principle could we move from running around on the ground to flying through the air in machines that would otherwise be forever earthbound.

Divine transformation is like that. The coming of Jesus into human history and into our lives by the Holy Spirit brought, as it were, a new form of locomotion. Before he comes, we walk.

Then everything changes. The power within us and among us begins to propel us on the ground and even through the air. The face of human history begins to be transformed.

The first stages of God's transformation are like propulsion on the ground. The steam engine, the automobile, even the race car— life is radically changed. But that's only the beginning, for there is divine lift. The engine is the Holy Spirit, and we go fast and far on the ground. But when spiritual wings are molded by the wisdom of God, we are thrust heavenward into a whole new dimension of corporate transformation. Not only individuals, but also families, communities, and nations are reshaped forever. Transformation in one family, large or small, is linked with transformation in another, and before we know it, one plus one equals ten! We're in the air.

It is nothing less than revolutionary in every sphere; sometimes we call it transformational community development. Jesus reshapes our politics, economics, faith, and fellowship—and we are lifted into a new dimension, from wheels on the ground to wings in the air.

We have only begun to see it. But in his grace, it's time for "wheels up."

WESTERN CHRISTIANS AND CHRISTENDOM

We are living, it is said, in a post-Christendom world. The old sacred union between church and state that was born at the time of the Roman emperor Constantine is gone. A western culture that was once thoroughly Christian is passing away and being replaced by secular humanism and multicultural pluralism.

What are the implications of this for western Christians in mission? For sure, we are in a new missionary situation. We cannot assume the state will reinforce Christian morality and worship. Anabaptist Christians often remind us that the true church in the West has always been in a missionary situation.

Yet we cannot deny that something fundamental is different today. The truth is that even Anabaptist Christians and other members of free churches have been nurtured and protected by western governments for the past two hundred years, beginning in the United States. As Lutheran brother Patrick Keifert reminded Lancaster Mennonite Conference leaders in an annual assembly, "The Amish are the darlings of the American legal system."

Keifert, a lawyer and theologian, appears to be right. And the reason is straightforward. The American Constitution was framed by European colonists, many of whom were members of free churches like the Baptists, Methodists, Mennonites, and Brethren—all of whom had rejected the state churches of Europe and had been in turn rejected by them. Even the state churches of Europe, such as the Lutherans or Anglicans, could no longer function effectively as state churches in the new world. So the American Constitution became, in a sense, the first authentic expression of those European free churches that stood at the fountainhead of global evangelicalism and that had been preceded by the Anabaptists and other medieval evangelical groups.

So is the United States Constitution a free church document? Certainly not on the face of it. Yet perhaps it is closer to that than we ever knew. Did the United States create its early governmental forms in part to harbor and nurture radical European Christianity and in the process create a new form of Christendom, unperceived to be such by the various expressions of European anti-Constantinian Christianity, including the descendants of Anabaptists?

Perhaps. If so, however, we cannot assume that even this form of free church Christendom will last forever. As western culture changes, documents such as the U. S. Constitution can be reinterpreted to serve new purposes. New challenges to biblical faith will emerge in the West as well as in other parts of the world.

Western Christians have indeed been defended and nurtured in the United States. For this we are grateful—though we have not been grateful enough. But it has never been a right of radical Christians to be loved by their neighbors. After all, Jesus told us the world would reject his followers.

What is true for all western Christians is also true for Anabaptists. With them, we are also walking toward our own post-Christendom. May we go with joy, full of faith and courage, whatever the future holds.

IS THERE HOPE FOR THE TRADITIONAL CHURCH?

The question rang in my ears, almost taking me off guard. "Do you at the mission board believe there is no hope for the traditional church?"

"Is there any doubt?" I thought. I responded passionately, but with only a fraction of what was stirring in my heart.

Of course there's hope. But it's more than hope. It's past performance, present reality, and future promise. For wherever Jesus stands among his people acknowledged as Lord, the glory and the power of God are unleashed.

Jesus does indeed stand among us, within the traditional churches of our confession and other confessional circles. There must be no question that there is hope. Why should the question even enter anyone's mind?

Indeed, my question is this: Is there hope anywhere else? There's more hope for the traditional church than there is for the great churchly institutions of the twentieth century—the mission boards, the schools, the service agencies, the hospitals, the mutual aid societies. Apart from spiritual vitality in the traditional churches, these all soon disappear.

One might ask, But what about the non-traditional churches, the house churches, the new church plants, the missional churches, the emerging churches, the renewal churches, the seeker-sensitive churches, the Vineyards? Isn't there more hope for them?

Not really. For all of these are simply growing-edge expressions of the traditional church itself, and all are rapidly themselves becoming traditional. In 1982 my wife, Jewel, and I visited one of the early services of what was to become the Anaheim Vineyard, the mother church of the Vineyard movement—decidedly non-traditional. Yet fewer than twenty years later in faraway China, we met two young members of that congregation who described it now as very traditional.

The Willow Creek Community Church near Chicago, the mother church of the seeker-sensitive movement in the United States, after only twenty-five years was being described as an American tradition.

My point is not to criticize these movements, but to recognize how quickly new traditions form and how all of these are themselves expressions of the traditional church. Or to put it another way, the church of Jesus Christ is by its very nature traditional, rooted in Calvary and Pentecost two thousand years ago. It matters little whether the particular local church is more or less traditional in human terms. What matters is, is Jesus there?

Is there hope for the traditional church? Absolutely. Is there hope anywhere else?

A Hurrah for Ethnic Churches

Multiculturalism is in. Diversity is a mantra. Globalization is a code word for the twenty-first century.

In contrast, the Greek root *ethno* seems now to appear most often in phrases like ethnic pride, ethnic violence, and ethnic hatred. The Cold War has passed into history, and in its place is an almost universal bewildering maze of ethnic tensions that rip apart the veneer of civility in societies everywhere—the Tutus and Hutus, the Irish and English, Serbs and Croats, Palestinian Arabs and Israeli Jews, European-Americans and African-Americans, Kikuyu and Luo, and on and on.

Our ethnicity is a good gift from God. Every nuclear or extended family is a new beginning of ethnicity. (Families become clans; clans become ethnic groups.) Every person born into the world becomes part of an ethnic group, with language, customs, and culture different from most other people.

Cultures emerge and disappear, but *culture* does not. As old ones die, new ones are formed.

All of us are in some sense prisoners of our culture. With great effort a few of us learn more than a half-dozen languages; a tiny circle in each generation learns twenty or thirty, but human lifetimes are not long enough to go much further, even for the most brilliant.

Christian congregations are not unlike individuals. Each has its own corporate culture. Each tends to reflect quite accurately one of the thousands of human ethnic groups. A few, of course, may learn five or ten languages, and these are called multicultural churches. But most are monocultural, reflecting one ethnic group.

It is time to accept and celebrate reality. Monocultural, ethnic congregations are okay. They are even beautiful, as African-Americans began to teach us in the 1960s.

To be specific, Swiss-German American or Dutch-Russian American traditional Anabaptist congregations are ethnic churches. Are they therefore bad? Only if loyalty to their particular form of ethnicity is elevated above loyalty to Jesus as Lord. That would be idolatry—ethnic idolatry.

On the other hand, replacing monoculturalism with multiculturalism does not automatically make a church better. In fact, it sometimes makes it worse. It is harder for leaders to be representative, for members to be understood, for unity to be achieved. Not impossible, just harder.

Of course, there are beautiful multicultural churches. May their tribes increase. And there are beautiful monocultural churches. May their tribe increase.

But at the end of the conversation we would have to reckon that the vast majority of Christian churches since Pentecost have been what we would call ethnic, monocultural churches. The critical issue is not, were they ethnic? Rather, it is, were they faithful?

Jesus, after all, was ethnic. So are all of us. Let's celebrate every ethnic form in which we come. It's God's good gift. Then even more, let's celebrate our oneness in Christ. God's greatest gift.

WHERE THE CHURCH IS NOT—YET

"'Not by might nor by power, but by my Spirit,' says the Lord" (Zechariah 4:6).

Zechariah's prophetic words gripped, challenged, and changed the participants in the 2007 International Missions Association events held in Bechterdissen, Germany. Eighty-six mission leaders and guests from twenty-five nations joined an equal number of local participants for an unforgettable encounter with five leaders of China's house church movement.

Peter Xu and Brother Yun, well-known elders in the movement, were joined by Brother Yun's wife and son, along with Deborah, a young evangelist and spiritual daughter of Xu, to weave a tapestry of testimony, story, and challenge that left us awed by God. The entire global mission network was humbled and stirred to new steps of obedience.

Brother Yun reported that in 1949 there were 800,000 Christians in China, but that today there may be 130 million. "It's a miracle of God," he said. "When the prison guards smashed my knees, they asked, 'How will you get there [west toward Jerusalem] if you can't walk?'

"But I believe from the bottom of my heart that Jesus did rise from the dead! In prison Satan almost succeeded in making me hopeless. Brothers and sisters outside also almost gave up hope. Neither great wealth nor great power could gain my release. But

God's actions are faster than our thoughts, faster than the fastest computer in the world.

"When I lay on the prison floor, God told me to get up and go out. At that very moment, Brother Xu laid his hand on the door of my cell from the other side, and it opened!"

In the next moments Brother Yun walked, free, out of that maximum-security prison. He continued:

"There are so many prisons in the world. I pray in every service that people will come out of their prisons. Let's make Satan angry by our joy! Every nation between China and Jerusalem will hear the gospel. We need the support of our European brothers and sisters because of their experience in the past. We join with Christians in every part of the world. We join with you.

"When I was put in prison after evading the police for many years, I said, 'Jesus, I'm in prison.' He said, 'I know.' Then he filled me with such joy that I couldn't contain it. The police thought I was crazy. I wanted to die for Jesus, and I almost did. When they finally brought my wife in to see me for the last time, she didn't even recognize me.

"But through prayer God opened the prison doors for me in China. Four iron doors opened before me. I had no keys. Outside the prison a taxi came immediately and picked me up. There in the taxi the Lord opened my eyes and I saw the Lamb of God standing with the keys of life and death.

"The Lord wants to open the doors of life and death in your country too. Through prayer he will open the door to the ends of the earth."[18]

It is the path ahead. As the Holy Spirit leads us, we are going to places where the church is not—yet.

This is not the lonely vision of some wild-eyed radical—unless, that is, we consider Jesus to be that. For Jesus' last words before ascending are directed precisely to all the "not yet" places of the world: "You will receive power ... and you will be my witnesses" (Acts 1:8).

Nor is it the exceptional vision of a few mission enthusiasts in contrast to what the Lord is stirring across the whole body of Christ. Everywhere the Holy Spirit is nudging us to reach beyond ourselves. This is a movement of the Spirit that goes far beyond the use of a few particular words or concepts or the vision of one Christian spiritual stream.

The language that fires our vision varies. In some circles it is the old-fashioned missionary church; in others it is the missional church; in still others, it is the cell church, the house church, or the seeker-sensitive church. It is easy to debate the differences and choose our favorites.

There are differences, to be sure. Yet underlying all of our attempts to "get it right" about how to do church, the movement of the Spirit keeps us reaching beyond ourselves to where Jesus is not yet known.

We live in a time of enormous, even cataclysmic, change. For more than five hundred years the western church has stretched by faith to those many frontiers where Jesus is little known, where the church is weak or nonexistent. The sixteenth-century Jesuit brothers like Ignatius Loyola, the eighteenth-century Moravians and Baptists, the nineteenth century evangelicals, and the twentieth-century Pentecostals—all have played a part. The sixteenth-century European radicals laid important spiritual foundations for all that followed them. This remains our guiding vision.

Now there is the enormous new missionary vision of the churches of Africa, Asia, and Latin America. In January 2008, at a meeting of a global mission network initiated by the *Centro Christiano Internacional* (CCI) in Tegucigalpa, Honduras, eighty-three congregations in twenty nations were represented, some of them working in the world's most difficult places to reach.

CCI is one of the granddaughter churches of our particular mission society, Eastern Mennonite Missions. It was born from the church of Living Love (*Amor Viviente*), which in turn was initiated under the leadership of Ed King, a North American missionary we sent. They and we together are blessed immensely by our continuing relationship.

Spiritual grandchildren, just like the natural ones, tend to be more different from their grandparents than were the children of those grandparents. Yet the DNA continues, and here in Honduras it is thrilling to see, even in the third generation, that same vision for going to places where the church is not—yet. At the CCI meeting, one of their leaders prayed, "Lord, we are unworthy, we are weak, we are not excellent, but we want to go."

May that be our prayer too. For we also as North American Christians are unworthy, weak, and not excellent. We struggle to hear, understand, and obey. We find it difficult to connect with each other, to support each other. But we are called and anointed to send and to go.

Not yet, but soon. Even so, come, Lord Jesus.

ACTIVITIES AND QUESTIONS FOR DISCUSSION

Part 1: The Vision

What is the vision or mission statement of your congregation? In what way does it incorporate both local and global missions?

Create a proposal for (a) incorporating global missions in a congregational vision/mission statement or (b) strengthening an already existing focus on global missions in such a statement.

Part 2: The People

Who are the people from your congregation currently serving as long-term, cross-cultural Christian witnesses? Who are those who have served during the past thirty years?

What congregational structures are in place for prayer, communication, and visits with these cross-cultural Christian witnesses? What could be done to improve them?

Create a definite plan of personal support and prayer for at least one cross-cultural witness whom you know. Invite others to join you.

Part 3: The Walk

Does your congregation have a well-defined way of partnering with a sister congregation in another country? This could take place through periodic pulpit exchanges, visits, correspondence, exchange of financial or personnel gifts, or friendships.

Create a proposal for (a) incorporating an international sister relationship for your congregation with at least one congregation in another country or (b) strengthening an already existing relationship with such a congregation.

Part 4: The World

What opportunities exist in your community for engaging people from other parts of the world—immigrants, students, visitors? List them.

Create a proposal for congregational global engagement through international connections in your home community.

Part 5: The Path Ahead

List ways you can be personally engaged in witness through local engagement in outreach or by learning from brothers and sisters in other parts of the world—whether going yourself or supporting others who go to places where the church is weak or nonexistent.

Create a plan that includes missions as an integral part of your life and in radical obedience to Jesus. Implement it, and review it weekly.

NOTES

1. Geoffrey Wainwright, *Lesslie Newbigin: A Theological Life*, (Oxford: Oxford University Press, 2000), p. 14.

2. Contemporary literature associated with the loose networks known as "missional church" or "emerging church" abounds. Darrell L. Guder has high name recognition associated with the missional church, Brian McLaren with the emerging church. A recent book on the missional church is *Treasure in Clay Jars: Patterns in Missional Faithfulness*, Lois Y. Barrett, ed., and Walter C. Hobbs, project leader, (Grand Rapids, MI: Eerdmans, 2004). On the emerging church, there is *Blue Like Jazz: Nonreligious Thoughts on Christian Spirituality*, by Donald Miller (Nashville: Thomas Nelson, 2003).

3. Ralph Winter, *Six Essential Components of World Evangelization: Goals for 1984*, (Pasadena, CA: William Carey Library, 1978), 3.

4. George Huntston Williams, *The Radical Reformation*, Philadelphia: Westminster Press, 1962, especially pp. 118-298; Franklin Hamlin Littell, *The Anabaptist View of the Church: An Introduction to Sectarian Protestantism*, American Society of Church History, 1952, especially pp. 94-99; John Howard Yoder, *The Politics of Jesus: Vicit Agnus Noster*, (Grand Rapids, MI: Eerdmans, 1972), especially 115-34, 193-214.

5. John Wesley, *The Works of John Wesley: Third Edition: Complete and Unabridged: Volume I: Journals from October 14, 1735 to November 29, 1745*, (Peabody, MA: Hendrickson, 1991), reprinted from the 1872 edition issued by Wesleyan Methodist Book Room, London, p. 22.

6. The Global Disciples Network has central offices in Lancaster, Pennsylvania, but staff and funding structures span the globe. There are plans to create an international board. The facilitator for the Global Discipleship Training Alliance is a keen Ethiopian mission leader, Tefera Bekere.

7. Lesslie Newbigin, *Foolishness to the Greeks: The Gospel and Western Culture*, (Grand Rapids, MI: Eerdmans, 1986), pp. 18-20.

8. David J. Bosch, *Transforming Mission: Paradigm Shifts in Theology of Mission*, (Maryknoll, NY: Orbis, 1991), 232.

9. Gregory Boyd, *God at War: The Bible and Spiritual Conflict*, (Downers Grove, IL: InterVarsity Press, 1997).

10. First Samuel 16:7 is a biblical illustration of "being before God." David was chosen king of Israel by no human criteria that distinguished him from his brothers. Rather, he was chosen because God saw his heart.

11. The "10/40 Window" is the region of the world from ten degrees to forty degrees north of the equator, stretching from West Africa to Southeast Asia. Here live more than 90% of the world's least-reached people groups, i.e., those who have no Christian neighbors.

12. David Ruis, *We Will Dance*, (Vineyard Music USA: Vineyard Publishing, 1993), Song Number 1034438.

13. See note 11.

14. Stephen Neill, *A History of Christian Missions: The Pelican History of the Church: 6*, (Baltimore: Penguin Books, Inc., 1964), pp. 69-77.

15. Patrick Keifert, a Lutheran scholar and proponent of missional church theology and practice, has served unofficially but effectively as a "bishop" to the Lancaster Mennonite Conference in early twenty-first century through his assistance as consultant, friendly critic, and insightful networker in promoting radical congregational revitalization for holistic local and global outreach.

16. For the story of John of Resh-aina and Thomas the Tanner, see Samuel Hugh Moffett, *A History of Christianity in Asia: Volume I: Beginnings to 1500: Second Edition*, (Maryknoll, New York: Orbis Books, 1998), pp. 208, 209. For the rest, see the standard western texts such as Stephen Neill, *A History of Christian Missions: The*

Pelican History of the Church: 6, (Baltimore: Penguin Books, 1964), pp. 52-53, 69-77, 84-88.

17. David Aikman, *Jesus in Beijing: How Christianity is Transforming China and Changing the Global Balance of Power*, (Washington, D.C.: Regnery Publishing , 2003); Brother Yun, Peter Xu Yongze and Enoch Wang with Paul Hattaway, *Back to Jerusalem: Called to Complete the Great Commission*, (Carlisle, U.K.: Piquant, 2003).

18. Quoted from the author's conference notes. For the whole story, read Brother Yun with Paul Hattaway, *The Heavenly Man: The Remarkable True Story of Chinese Christian Brother Yun*, (Grand Rapids, MI: Monarch Books, 2002).

THE AUTHOR

Richard Showalter is president of Eastern Mennonite Missions. He has served as a missionary in the Middle East and Kenya, and as a church planter in Ohio. Showalter was president of Rosedale Bible College from 1989 to 1994 and remains an adjunct faculty member. He holds graduate degrees from University of Chicago Divinity School, Associated Mennonite Biblical Seminary, and Gordon-Conwell Theological Seminary. Showalter lives in Landisville, Pennsylvania, and is a member of West End Mennonite Fellowship.